# A Handbook of Wrestling
# Terms and Holds

Also by Thompson Clayton:

*Wrestling for Boys*
*Living and Understanding*
*An Introduction to Wrestling*
*Wrestling for Fun*

# A Handbook of Wrestling

# Terms and Holds

*New and Revised Edition*

Compiled by Thompson Clayton with the help of

Doug Parker, Springfield College •
Charlie Speidel, Penn State University •
Rex Peery, University of Pittsburgh •
Joe Begala, Kent State University •
Arnold W. Umbach, Alabama Poly •
Cliff Keen, University of Michigan •
Fendley Collins, Michigan State University •
Dave McCuskey, University of Iowa •
Keith Bowen, Montana State College •
Karl Kitt, U.S. Air Force Academy •
Dr. Stanley W. Henson, Jr., Fort Collins •
Jim Schall, Kelso High School, Washington •

South Brunswick
New York: A. S. Barnes and Company
London: Thomas Yoseloff Ltd

A. S. Barnes and Co., Inc.,
Cranbury, New Jersey 08512


Thomas Yoseloff Ltd
108 New Bond Street
London W1Y OQX, England


ISBN 0-498-01340-5
Printed in the United States of America

# Contents

# Foreword

The idea of compiling a handbook of wrestling terms has probably been in the minds of many coaches. When this idea first came to me more than ten years ago, I was struggling vainly to interpret the writings of a Midwestern coach. His nomenclature was so different from mine that I could get next to nothing from his description of maneuvers. Other potentially valuable material in the same publication, the old *AWCOA Bulletin*, was likewise nearly useless. If I could learn the name used for a certain hold in all sections of the country then all I would need to do to understand what a coach was talking about would be to refer to the name commonly used in his section. With this idea in mind I sent out an appeal for help to some of the leading coaches in all sections of the United States. The response was better than I had any reason to expect. As a result of this I mailed out questionnaires to the fifteen listed below:

Doug Parker, Springfield College
Charlie Speidel, Penn State University
Rex Peery, University of Pittsburgh
Joe Begala, Kent State University
Arnold W. Umbach, Alabama Poly
Cliff Keen, University of Michigan
Fendley Collins, Michigan State University
Port G. Robertson, University of Oklahoma
Dave McCuskey, University of Iowa
Keith Bowen, Montana State College
Karl Kitt, U.S. Air Force Academy
Ray Jenkins, University of Colorado
Dr. Stanley W. Henson, Jr., Fort Collins
Bill Tomaras, Washington State College
Jim Schall, Kelso High School, Wash.

At the same time—in the early part of 1958—I started a binder of some 387 drawings of numbered holds. It had been my original intention to send separate copies to each coach but duplication problems forced me to give up this idea. The binder required more than three years to make the rounds of the coaches. At one time it seemed lost somewhere in transit and I had visions of several-hundred hours of work gone up in smoke. Added to this, questionnaires from three of the fifteen coaches never reached me. Rather than to send out more questionnaires and ask them to do the job over, I determined to go ahead with the material received from the remaining twelve.

A change of jobs, graduate study, and overtime work further delayed work until the summer of 1963 when I began to work on the glossary. Three weeks of intermittent work convinced me that my original idea was impractical. A complete glossary of terms might well run to a hundred pages and still not serve the purpose for which it was intended. I had discovered that terminology was not sectionally oriented. It was more of an individual situation. At this point it seemed sensible to stop and reexamine the whole project. In 1959 I was appointed by Dr. Frank Finger, then president of the AWCOA, to attempt beginning a standardization of wrestling nomenclature. The committee of which I was the chairman was to meet at the NCAA championships at the University of Iowa. Unfortunately, the date of the meeting came on the same day that I was to start at a new teaching position in Maine. As it turned out, I was able to get Doug Parker to take over for me, and a meeting was held at which he presided. At this meeting, the coaches were in agreement that rather than to try to adopt a standard term for every move and counter move, it would be better to start with a few basic moves upon which they could all agree. From this point, progress in naming holds should proceed with caution. As the questionnaires had not all been returned at this time Doug Parker was not furnished with lists from which proposed names might be selected.

Some suggestions and criticisms from participating coaches have been helpful in directing further efforts toward both the establishment of a standard nomenclature and the compilation of an encyclopedia. One of these was that descriptive, rather than pet, or catchy, names be used. Another suggestion was that because some of the maneuvers shown are fundamentally unsound an expert group should be selected to eliminate these.

With the first suggestion in mind, I went about examining the questionnaires to determine which names were (1) most descriptive (2) most widely used. There were problems. Almost every coach in the country knows what the whizzer is. Yet this name is not descriptive. "Overarm hook" is a far more descriptive term. In this instance, it seemed preferable to use "Whizzer." In some instances, no truly descriptive term was submitted. In these instances, I referred back to the best previous descriptive terms for similar moves to coin a name. It was difficult at first to concede that an unfamiliar term was superior to one which I had been using for 30 or 40 years. Yet, in the process of selecting the best terms from those that were submitted—"Japanese armlock," "Princeton lock," "Japanese leg trip,"—"Mepham," and other favorites have gone by the board.

Concerning unsound holds, I found myself at odds with the thinking of some. My concept of an encyclopedia was one which showed all holds—good, bad, and indifferent. It is true that, according to the fundamentals of "control" wrestling, some of the maneuvers shown would be too risky, especially under the present rules. However, when we speak of "sound" moves, do we not speak of moves which are difficult to counter? And, since all moves may be countered, where do we stop cutting when we begin to cut out those that are risky? Furthermore, since the purpose of this encyclopedia is to provide a common language for coaches, are not names for unsound moves as necessary as names for sound moves?

The selection of one name for each maneuver reduces the glossary to a workable size. If it seems an arbitrary step, remember that the selected name in almost every instance is one contributed by one or more of the twelve coaches who returned the best of those submitted by our experts.

# Acknowledgments

I wish to express my sincere thanks to the individuals and publishers who have granted me use of their excellent new material:

To John Gorsuch, Wm. C. Brown Company, Publishers, for Arnold W. Umbach and Warren R. Johnson, *Successful Wrestling: Its Bases and Problems.* 2nd ed. (Dubuque, Iowa: Wm. C. Brown Company, 1972).

Ray F. Carson and Buel R. Patterson, *Principles of Championship Wrestling.* (South Brunswick, New Jersey: A. S. Barnes and Company, 1972). By permission of the publisher.

George Gianakaris, *Action Drilling in Wrestling.* (South Brunswick, New Jersey: A. S. Barnes and Company, 1969).

Richard C. Maertz, *Wrestling Techniques: Takedowns.* (South Brunswick, New Jersey: A. S. Barnes and Company, 1970).

I also thank Arnold W. Umbach for supplying valuable photographic assistance with new materials, and the following coaches for their assistance in the naming of holds:

Doug Parker, Springfield College
Charlie Speidel, Pennsylvania State University (retired)
Rex Peery, University of Pittsburgh
Joe Begala, Kent State University (retired)
Arnold W. Umbach, Auburn University
Cliff Keen, University of Michigan (retired)
Fendley Collins, Michigan State University (retired)
Dave McCuskey, University of Iowa (retired)
Karl Kitt, U. S. Air Force
Jim Schall, Kelso High School, Washington
Ed Peery, U. S. Naval Academy

# Wrestling Terms

Wrestling terms are used by people who understand what they mean but the same terms may have a different meaning to others. Some of these are bar, lock, check, block, lever, grapevine, scissor.

A "bar" is usually thought of as the mechanical placing of an object in such a way as to prevent further movement in one direction. A "lock" is construed to mean the prevention of further movement by a part of the body in any direction. For example: headlock, armlock, wristlock, bodylock. A "check" is used interchangeably sometimes with "bar" or "block." A "block" means any move which interferes with the execution of another. A "lever" implies a mechanical advantage having a lever and a fulcrum. The so-called headlever, or arm lever, uses the top of the head as a fulcrum. Yet some holds are termed levers which do not have a fulcrum and some that do have fulcrums are not termed levers. A scissor hold, for example, has a double fulcrum; that is, each leg has a fulcrum. A "grapevine" usually refers to the entwining action of one leg around the other. But there are also arm "grapevines" such as the one-arm wristlock. Actually, the familiar "scissor" is much more like the action of a nutcracker since its power is derived from two different points rather than one.

Many holds, such as the familiar double bar, or double arm pry, are really levers. Thus, it can be seen that the naming of moves has been very unsystematic and needs a lot of study. However, no such ambitious and iconoclastic undertaking is intended in this work. It seems sufficient to provide an understanding of the language as it is used and to help establish a standard nomenclature.

# A Handbook of Wrestling
# Terms and Holds

# Note

The following section contains a listing of the various names used for 445 maneuvers, along with an illustration of each. The illustrations are captioned with the most popular name of the maneuver.

# Wrestling Nomenclature and Illustrations

1. Double leg tackle
   Lifting man thru on double leg pull up
   Leg dive
   Double leg drop
   Double leg tackle—kneeling

Double leg tackle

Sprawl

2. Sprawl counter for double leg tackle
   Sprawling to prevent double leg pull up
   Dropping the boom on the sprawl
   Double leg drift
   Sprawl with over arm lock
   Sprawl or shoot legs back
   Hiplock counter
   Move legs back to counter double leg drop
   Sprawl (block)
   Sprawl

3. Double winglock roll
   Back winging
   Double arm lock with head drag
   Double reverse wing
   Reverse wing lock standing
   Duck under arm
   Reverse winglock
   Reverse double wing back
   Duck under

Double reverse wing

13

4. Underhook and stiff arm counter for No. 1
   Lever block for double leg tackle
   Bar arm and inside crotch check
   Sprawl with under arm lock
   Single bar over back
   Arm lock and inside crotch
   Move feet back, single bar and groin pry to
        counter double leg drop
   Extended whizzer

Underhook and
inside thigh block

Reverse wing and
elbow lock

5. Double arm lock roll as counter for No. 4
   Back wing
   Double arm lock, set through head drag
   Head under with single arm wing
   Reverse wing lock
   Double wing lock
   Reverse wing and elbow lock
   Reverse single wing
   Reverse side roll

6. Cross face and outside crotch counter for No. 1
   Sprawl and cross face
   Cross face and back crotch block of double
        leg tackle
   Cross face with over crotch check
   Cross face
   Cross face and rear crotch
   Cross face, rear catch to counter double leg drop
   Cross face and crotch
   Cross face—grab tail
   Cross face and tail (counter)

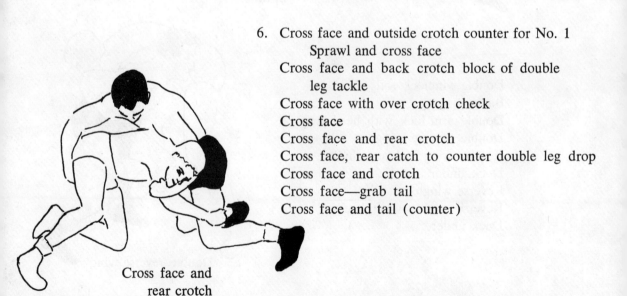

Cross face and
rear crotch

7. Quarter nelson counter for double leg tackle
   Quarter nelson (leg attack counter)
   Quarter nelson block of double leg tackle
   Quarter nelson
   Reverse quarter nelson
   Quarter nelson from the front
   Front 3/4 nelson
   3/4 nelson (counter)

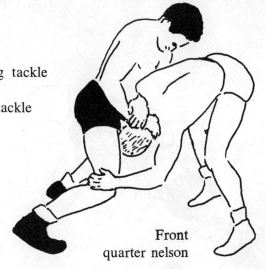

Front
quarter nelson

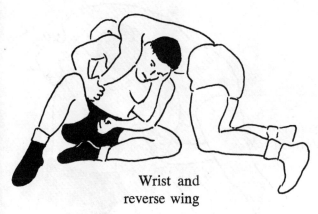

Wrist and
reverse wing

8. Under arm spin
   Back wing
   Double arm bar to pancake
   Head under arm and reverse single wing
   Reverse winglock—variation
   Sit into head drag
   Wrist and reverse wing
   Reverse single wing back
   Reverse side roll
   Arm hook and roll (counter)

9. Double underhook block for double
      leg tackle
   Under-cupping of arms
   Double arm bar, block for tackle
   Double arm check
   Sprawl with double under arm lock
   Double bar over back
   Arm Lock
   Double bar
   Under arm block
   Double shoulder block

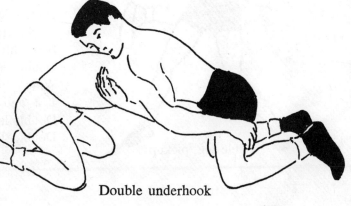

Double underhook

15

10. Double armlock roll—follow-up block
    for No. 1
    Back wing
    Double elbow tie up for set through
    Under arm double wing spinner
    Reverse wing lock—variation
    Sit through double bar over back
    Double elbow lock
    Double elbow lock and sit through
    Tip

Double
elbow lock

11. Fireman's lift (barrel roll)
    Fireman's carry with inside crotch lever
    Under arm lateral drop with crotch
    Fireman's carry (variation)
    Fireman's carry
    Double underarm block

Fireman's carry

12. Double leg tackle pickup
    Double leg pickup
    Body lift resulting from deep tackle
    Double leg pickup
    Wing
    1/2 and crotch in the air
    Double leg tackle with lift
    Double leg tackle—standing

Double leg pickup

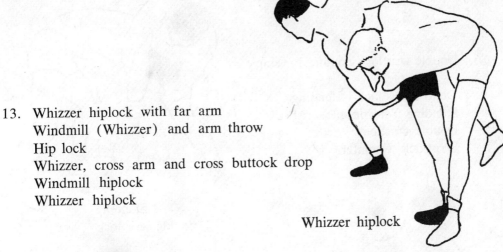

13. Whizzer hiplock with far arm
    Windmill (Whizzer) and arm throw
    Hip lock
    Whizzer, cross arm and cross buttock drop
    Windmill hiplock
    Whizzer hiplock

Whizzer hiplock

14. Reverse double bar lock (illegal)
    Double bar arm lock
    Double arm bar to pancake
    Double bar arm
    Double bar lock
    Locked double bar over back
    Double arm lock
    Double bar
    Front double arm bar

Double bar armlock

15. Single leg pickup head outside
    Single leg pickup
    Inside leg pickup (single)
    Single leg
    Single leg tackle

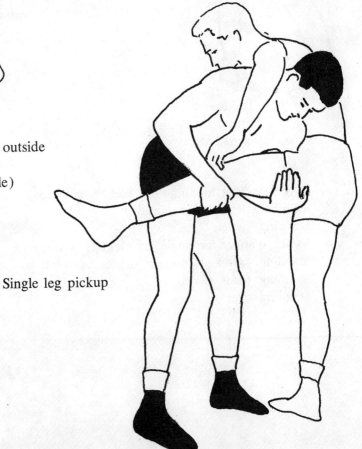

Single leg pickup

16. Double wristlock counter for single
       leg tackle
    Double wristlock—standing
    Standing front double wristlock
    Double wristlock
    Wristlock (counter)

Standing
double wristlock

Inside-out
counter for
double wristlock

17. Arm leverage block for double wristlock
    Hand lock (countering wristlock)
    Countering double wristlock
    Lock hands, pulling wristlock inside
    Double handgrip
    Arm lock counter for double wristlock
    Standing "inside-out" double wristlock counter
    Break for double wristlock
    Turning wristlock inside out

18. Switch counter for single leg pickup and trip
    Switching leg pickup (inside)
    Standing switch
    Switch counter for single leg pickup
    Standing switch (Counter single leg pickup)
    Standing front switch
    Standing over switch

Standing switch

19. Re-switch
   Re-switching (countering counter)
   Counter switch for switch
   Re-switch to counter standing front switch
   Run around switch

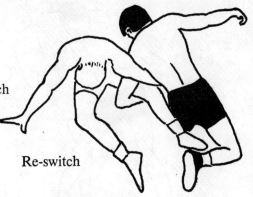

Re-switch

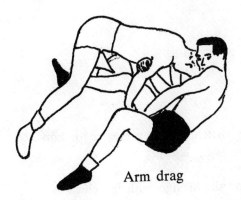

Arm drag

20. Arm drag counter for single leg pickup
   Arm dragging in countering No. 15
   Arm drag
   Under arm drag with leg elevator
   Set through drag
   Sitting Arm Drag

21. Re-drag
   Follow-up of No. 20 (leg cover)
   Preparing to re-drag the drag
   Underarm drag for lateral roll
   Step-over arm drag
   Counter drag

Re-drag

Single leg
pickup and trip

22. Single leg pickup and trip
Leg pickup and inside trip
Single leg trip from standing in front
Single leg pickup and back trip
Inside back heel trip
Inside leg trip
Inside leg pickup with backheel
Single leg tackle and backheel

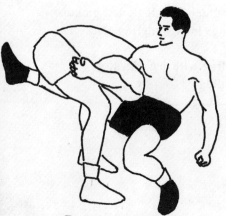

Reverse bar arm
with elevator

23. Arm grapevine switch, counter for leg pickup
Armlock switch with leg lift
Standing switch
Reverse arm bar sit through with leg elevator
Single wristlock standing
Arm hook variation of standing front switch
Switch leverage—step through

24. Waist lock and hip throw
Lateral drop with back leg trip
Standing hiplock trip
Standing, arm grasp with lateral
back leg trip
Body chancery with back heel
Back heel trip
Hip lock or back heel trip from hip
lock position
Back heel trip (arm & waist)

Body chancery
with back leg trip

20

25. Arm lock and hip throw
    Standing arm wing and back trip
    Arm lever standing hip-lock trip
    Standing, cross-arm drag with lateral
        back-leg trip
    Arm lock with back heel
    Variation of flying mare
    Back heel trip (arm)

Flying mare variation
with back trip

Waist and hiplock

26. Waist and hiplock
    Cross buttocks body lift
    Hiplock
    Standing cross arm with cross buttocks throw
    Headlock
    Arm and waist (hiplock)

27. Single leg tackle below the knee
    Low heel tackle and shoulder drive
    Single leg drop head outside (major error)
    Ankle with knee buck drop
    Single leg dive
    Knee lock
    Single leg tackle
    Knee breaker

Single leg dive
with shoulder drive

21

Bar arm and
chancery

28. Head chancery and arm bar takedown
    Bar arm and chancery
    Head overlock with pancake position
    Reverse bar arm and head chancery
    Head chancery and bar
    Front chancery and arm lock
    Under arm with head chancery
    Over and under

29. Crotch lift counter for head chancery
        and arm bar
    Set thru for pancake
    Bar arm with neck yoke, on mat, counter
    Head dragging (head chancery and bar)
    Arm lock, sit thru and body press
    Fall back

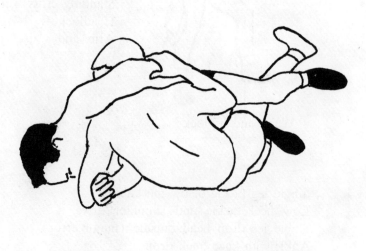

Rolling counter for
bar & chancery

30. Reverse double arm bar
    Elevator, set thru to overhead double
        arm tieup
    Double bar arm, sit back with stretcher to
        stretcher lock
    Double bar arm and sit thru

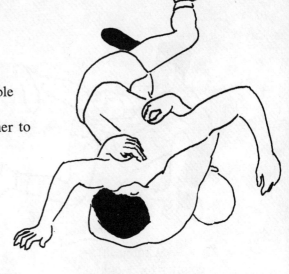

Elevator and
double arm
bar counter

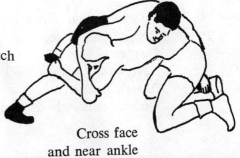

Cross face
and far ankle

31. Cross face and far ankle block for No. 1
    Cross face and far ankle
    Sprawl with cross face and far ankle
    Sprawl and cross face

32. Cross face and near ankle
    Sprawl with cross face and back crotch
    Cross face, near ankle check
    Cross face and near leg
    Cross face sprawl and near ankle

Cross face
and near ankle

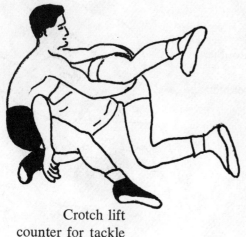

Crotch lift
counter for tackle

33. Crotch lift counter for leg tackle
Thigh lift (counter for leg attack)
Set through with leg pull
Crotch pickup check
Leg lift

Near ankle counter
for tackle

34. Near ankle lock counter for leg tackle
Near ankle grab
Near ankle pickup check
Knee lock
Single leg lift
Twisting knee lock
Near leg lift after moving legs back to
counter drop

35. Quarter nelson block for leg dive
Reverse half nelson and wrist
Quarter nelson
Reverse half nelson check
Reverse quarter nelson—variation
Quarter nelson from front

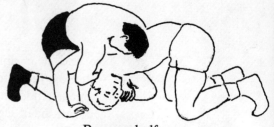

Reverse half—
quarter nelson

36. Fireman's carry takedown
    Tieup for fireman's carry (barrel roll)
    Head under arm drop or fireman's carry
    Under arm and crotch lateral takedown
    Head under arm sit through
    Fireman's carry

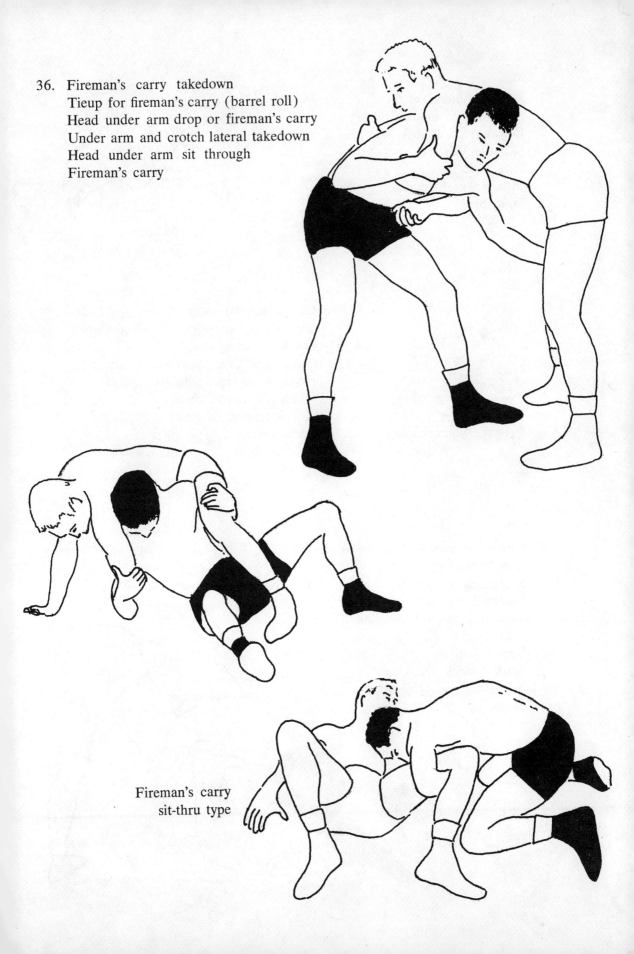

Fireman's carry
sit-thru type

37. Sprawl counter for fireman's carry
    Sprawling on fireman's carry
    Leg drift check to lateral near ankle pickup
    Shoot legs back or sprawl
    Arm lock
    Moved legs to counter
    Drag back

Sprawl counter for
fireman's carry

Pancake counter for
sprawl

38. Underarm and waist
    Counter for sprawl with lateral drop
    Fireman's carry
    Cross arm drag from lateral drive
    Head under arm (with arm pull)
    Fireman's carry whizzer
    Arm lock and far arm
    Variation of Kelly
    Yale counter

39. Single leg sweep—head-on inside
    Outside leg grab
    Single leg drop with head in front (correct)
    Lateral leg drop
    Single leg tackle—variation
    Single leg dive
    Leg pickup
    Start of single leg drop
    Single leg tackle
    Single leg

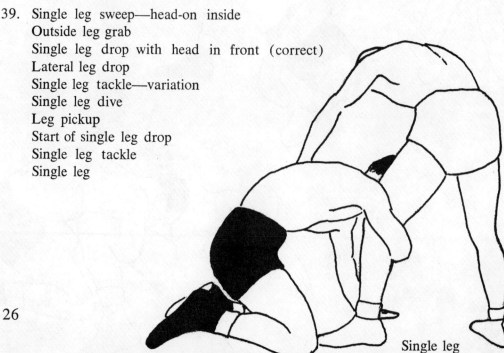

Single leg

40.  Back sweep escape double ankle hold

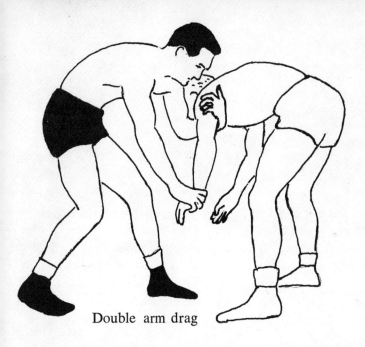

Double arm drag

41. Start of arm drag
    Arm drag
    Cross arm drag standing
    Double arm drag
    Standing, double arm drag
    Standing arm drag

42. Cross body block for arm drag
    Cross body block and trip
    Stepping over arm drag
    Cross block with back leg trip
    Cross body block
    Outside trip
    Back heel and cross body to counter arm drag
    Side—block counter (drag)
    Side body block

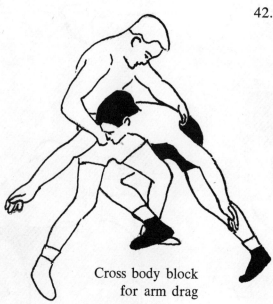

Cross body block
for arm drag

43. Hand on thigh counter for arm drag
    Crowding a drag with head bore
    Blocking arm drag with position of head
    Cross arm drag drifting under free arm
    Block with hand on hip
    Double arm drag
    Countering arm drag with head
    Head block counter (drag)
    Drag back

Head block counter
to arm drag

44. Arm drag—sit through
    Arm drag and leg catch
    Set down arm drag
    Under near arm drag and lateral knee
    Arm drag—variation
    Falling arm drag
    Double arm drag
    Falling, single arm drag and knee
    Arm Drag—step through

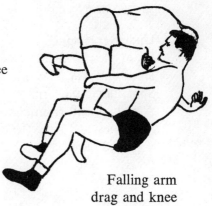

Falling arm
drag and knee

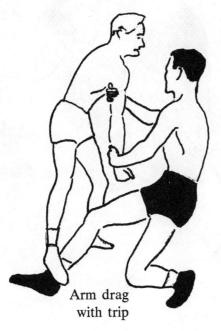

Arm drag
with trip

45. Arm drag pull by
    Arm drag with leg kick
    Foot trip arm drag
    Cross arm drag, lateral trip
    Arm drag—variation
    Arm drag with trip
    Double arm drag

46. Stepover counter for arm drag
    Straddle over sit through
    Cross body block
    Drag stepover (counter)
    Drag back—step across

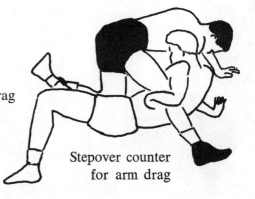

Stepover counter
for arm drag

47. Under arm spin
    Front view arm and chancery
    Head under arm sit through (variation)
    Spin under the arm
    Arm lock and front chancery
    Arm lock and spin (to counter chancery
        and bar)

Under arm spin

48. Head and far heel
    Whip-over (counter for inside leg attack)
    Cross ankle pickup
    Neck and ankle drop (far leg)
    Under arm Whizzer
    Cross leg pickup
    Cross ankle pickup
    Cross heel pickup
    Forward head and heel (right)
    Neck and far ankle
    Head and heel (far ankle)

Cross heel pickup

49. Head and near heel
    Cross over leg pickup from standing (locked)
    Come-on leg pickup
    Neck and ankle drop (near leg)
    Head and near ankle pickup
    Near leg pickup
    Near ankle pickup
    Near heel pickup
    Forward head and heel (left)
    Neck and near ankle
    Head and heel (near ankle)

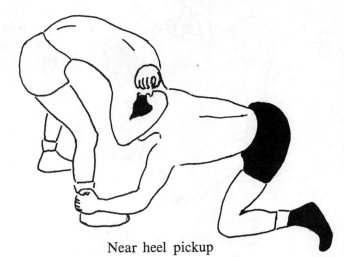

Near heel pickup

Pancake counter for
heel pickup

50. Pancake counter for head & heel takedown
    Arm lift counter for cross ankle pickup
    Block for neck & ankle drop—
        bar arm & cross arm drag
    Single bar & spike opposite arm
    Over & under

31

51. Elbow shove by counter for heel pickup

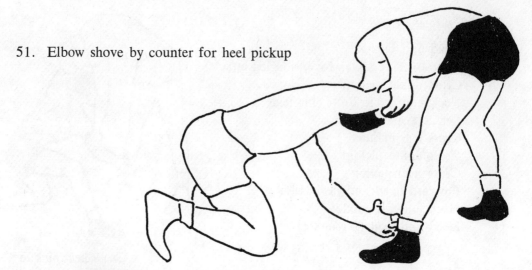

52. Under arm sneak
Under arm sweep
Set up for under near arm go behind
Duck under
Head drag

Under arm sneak
from elbow tieup

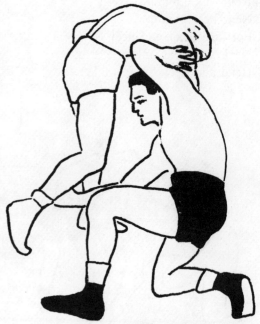

Arm throw-by
and ankle pickup

53. Arm lead and push to leg pickup
Arm throw and inside pickup
Over head drag
Under near arm to near leg drop
Arm throw-by and leg pickup
Drag by
Short arm drag
Combination duck under and single leg drop
Elbow throw by with ankle pickup
Elbow lift—catch ankle
Ankle pickup

32

54. Winglock cross over counter for head drag
    Winging a far arm reach of opponent
    Wing down and step over arm sweep
    Arm wing and step over
    Slip or duck under arm
    Near wing
    Near wing and step over
    Wing and step over

Wing and step over
counter for
under arm sneak

55. Side head lock
    Arm and chancery with cross buttocks
    Headlock with arm included hip throw
    Headlock and cross buttock throw
    Side headlock with arm
    Head lock
    Arm and head hiplock

Hiplock, arm and head

56. Leg grapevine counter for side head lock
    Grapevine to prevent cross buttocks
    Grapevine on far leg to counter head
        lock throw
    Leg grapevine to cross body ride
    Cross body to counter headlock
    Grapevine leg
    Grapevine
    Grapevine block

Grapevine counter
for headlock

33

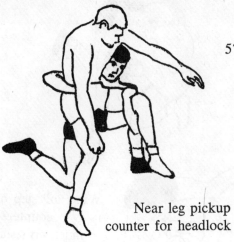

Near leg pickup
counter for headlock

57. Near leg pickup, counter for headlock
    Thigh pickup
    Leg lift
    Drop behind leg pickup
    Rear body lock with lift at hock of knee
    Rear pickup
    Near leg pickup
    Body hold, near leg lift and backward trip
    Under leg and hiplock (against stand-up)
    Fall back—near leg

58. Forward trip counter for side headlock
    Waist lock and cross trip
    Near leg forward trip
    Lateral leg trip
    Rear body lock with outside leg trip
    Pull head out
    Outside leg trip
    Forward trip

Forward trip
counter for headlock

Navy ride
with backward drop
counter for headlock

59. Navy Ride and backward drop counter
        for side headlock
    Inside crotch (counter chancery)
    Back heel trip set down
    Cross crotch pickup from behind
    Rear bodylock and sit back
    Inside crotch pickup
    Body hold, far leg lift and backward trip
    Fall back—far leg

60. Limp arm counter for whizzer
    Step behind
    Hip lock counter removing arm
    Drop to fours—leg behind leg check
    Step behind
    Arm push and step behind near leg

Step behind
counter for under
arm sneak

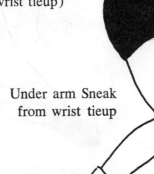

61. Under arm sneak
    Arm lift and head under arm sneak
    Under arm sweep
    Head under, arm lift—go behind
    Duck under (from wrist tieup)
    Head drag

Under arm Sneak
from wrist tieup

Standing step behind
switch

62. Standing winglock
    Wing switch and trip
    Standing step behind switch
    Lateral reverse arm wing, sit through
    Combination switch and side roll
    Spin behind head drag
    Winglock
    Inside switch and roll combination
    Rolling switch (standing)

35

Scissors leg trip

63. Step over leg lock
    Double leg scissors trip
    Single leg scissors kick take down
    Hindu trip

64. Lateral drop
    Standing lateral drop
    Over and under lateral drop with foot trip
    Whizzer
    Fast back drop

Lateral drop

65. Under arm and inside leg takedown
    No. 2 position of Fireman's carry
    Fireman's carry
    Under arm lateral pickup

Fireman's carry
rocker type

Head pull and
leg pickup

66. Collar and leg sweep
    Outside swing to leg pickup
    Side leg pickup
    Lateral drop with knee pickup
    The merry-go-round
    Single leg pickup
    Near leg pickup
    Head pull and leg drop combination
    Swinging knee pickup
    Neck and near leg pickup

67. Arm drag to backward trip
    Fake arm drag and leg trip
    Arm drag with back heel trip
    Near arm drag with inside trip
    Arm drag with inside back heel
    Double arm drag trip
    Fake arm drag and inside back heel trip
    Reverse drag and trip

Arm drag with inside
back heel

68. Double ankle pull
    Ankle and inside leg trip (with hand)
    Single legdrop with ankle squeeze trip
    Near ankle drop with cross trip
    Single leg tackle completed with double
        ankle pull
    Double leg tackle variation
    Double ankle pickup
    Completion of single leg drop
    Near and far ankle

Ankle (double) trip
with hands

Over and under tieup

69. Over and under tieup position
    Under arm tieup
    Start of kipup swing
    Locked horns to under arm
    Slip under arm
    Arm lift
    Arm bar lift
    Elbow and under arm tieup
    Under arm grab

70. Collar and triceps tieup position
    Elbow push up
    Start of overhead drag
    Shot put lift on near arm
    Slip under arm variation
    Arm lift
    Elbow lift
    Neck and elbow tieup

Collar and triceps tieup

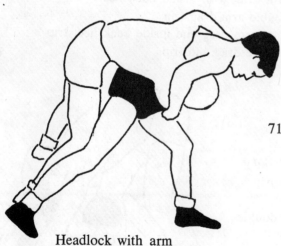

71. Side headlock
    Side chancery and arm
    Headlock with one arm included
    Side headlock with arm
    Country hiplock

Headlock with arm

72. Flying mare
    Front wing
    Flying mare with knee drop

Flying mare

73. Head chancery and inside crotch lift
    Half nelson and crotch from standing
    Start of head over lock set through
    Neck yoke and inside crotch pickup
    Half nelson and crotch
    Duck under, head chancery, crotch lift
            combination
    Chancery and lift

Half nelson and
crotch from standing

74. Reverse double bar and backward trip
    Double bar arm and cross trip
    Double over head bar with hip-lock trip
    Double bar arm with back leg trip
    Double bar over back with outside heel
            trip (back)
    Double arm lock and trip
    Double bar and in back heel trip

Double bar with
back leg trip

75. Double leg tackle and backward trip
    Double leg capture with back heel trip
    Tackle with leg trip
    Double leg pickup with back heel
    Outside trip
    Set back
    Double leg drop and outside back heel trip

Double leg tackle with
back trip

76. Snap down
    Head snap
    Head snap down check
    Slap down
    Snap down from knees
    Reverse head bar with drag

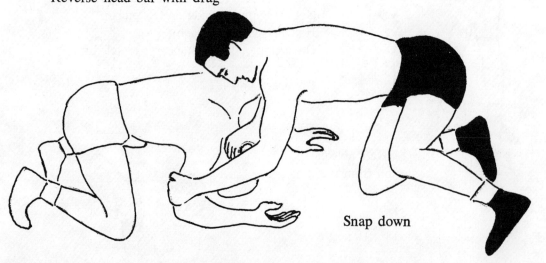

Snap down

77. Elbow hook counter for snap down
    Close tieup from kneeling facing position
    Countering snap down
    Head snap down check
    Knees under to prevent slap down
    Counter to slap down (arm rest)
    Over arm hook to block snap down
    Tieup on knees

Elbow hook to
counter slap down

Whizzer and
ankle pickup

78. Arm lock and heel pickup
    Whizzer and ankle pickup
    Leg lift to set down from hip lock position
    Reverse, inside ankle pickup
    Arm lock and heel pickup
    Pickup inside foot with windmill
    Hiplock and ankle pickup
    Inside leg pickup from whizzer position
    Whizzer and ankle drop back
    Whizzer and pull leg through

79. Chin Push
    Face shove
    Near elbow drag and chin push
    Head throw by
    Straighten opponent up for inside crotch
          pickup
    Short arm drag, head shove
    Chin push and arm drop to inside crotch
    Arm throw to crotch lift with push

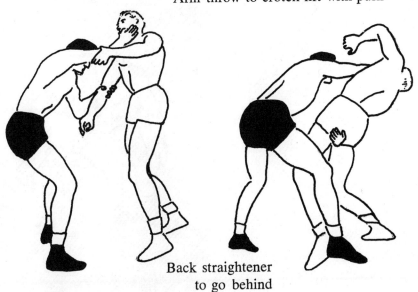

Back straightener
to go behind

80. Whizzer with grapevine for fallback

81. Heel pickup counter for standing whizzer

82. Hock lift counter for standing whizzer

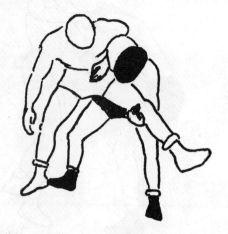

83. Whizzer throw with inside grapevine and
far elbow

84. Outside leg trip from rear standing
Cross leg trip
Forward trip
(standing) leg grapevine trip forward
Rear bodylock with outside trip
Forward trip
Outside leg trip
Forward trip
Rear hug and trip
Waist lock and grapevine

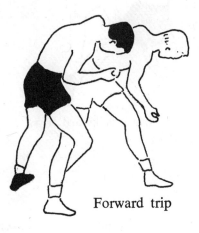

Forward trip

85. Switch counter for waist lock from
rear standing
Standing-sitting switch
Sit out standing switch
Switch set up
Standing switch
Switch

Standing switch
countering waist hold

86. Switch counter for outside leg trip from
        rear standing
    Covering leg to counter switch movement
    Short switch
    Switch from underneath, leg inside
    Standing switch
    Switch
    Inside switch

Switch
countering
forward trip

Crossover backward trip

87. Cross over from rear standing
    Fall back take to mat
    Cross thigh back trip
    Crossover back heel
    Crossback heel trip
    Crossover
    Crossover backward trip
    Rear cross drop
    Cross back heel

88. Switch as counter for crossover

89. Knee bend take back from rear standing
    Knee hock brace and waist lock takedown
    Knee break for fall back
    Heel to knee hock back trip
    Back heel
    Break knee down
    Knee kick
    Backward trip with near knee block
    Rear knee drop

Backward trip with
knee block

90. Leg pickup escape from rear standing
    Catching opponent's leg between legs
    Leg lift to set back to cradle
    Reverse inside ankle pickup
    Heel grab and knee lock
    Pickup heel from inside
    Inside leg pickup
    Inside leg pickup to reverse opp. standing
        behind
    Ankle pull through
    Reach through to ankle

Heel pickup
through legs

Double wrist hold
as counter for
heel pickup

91. Wrist pull counter for No. 90
    Catching def. man's hands between legs
    Countering leg lift set back
    Double wrist pickup
    Grab hands as counter for No. 90
    Double wrist grab
    Double wrist hold

92. Back heel counter for No. 90
    Blocking leg lift set back
    Foot to heel block
    Block foot outside as counter for No. 10
    Counter to leg pickup
    Inside leg pickup to counter backward trip
        (wrong picture?)
    Rear heel drop

Back heel as
block for heel pickup

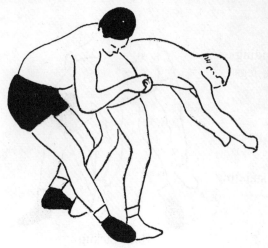

93. Back heel from rear standing
    Single back-heeling
    Fall back take to the mat
    Back heel trip
    Back heel
    Heel block and backward trip
    Rear single heel drop

Single back heel

94. Back heel from rear standing
    Double back heeling
    Fall back take to the mat
    Double back heel trip
    Back heel
    Double heel block and backward trip
    Rear double heel drop

Double back heel

95. Double leg drop from rear standing
    Dropping to shins and shoulder drive
    Shoulder drive take to mat
    Double ankle and buttocks buck
    Double ankle grab
    Dump forward grasping both ankles
    Double leg pickup
    Rear shoulder nudge
    Ankles and tail lift

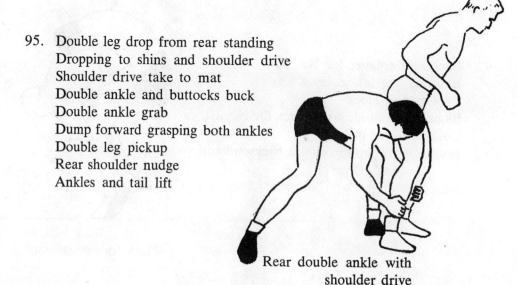

Rear double ankle with
shoulder drive

96. Near leg pickup and forward trip
    Leg pickup and inside leg trip (from rear)
    Single leg trip
    Single leg pickup and inside leg trip
    Grab ankle and trip
    Pickup ankle with outside trip
    Inside leg trip
    Waist and Clobber trip
    Snow Plow

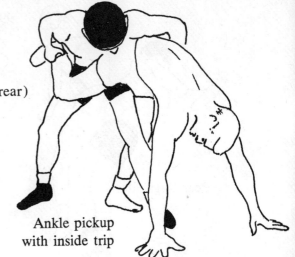

Ankle pickup
with inside trip

97. Far leg pickup from rear standing
    Reverse thigh lift
    High crotch lift
    Rear cross crotch pickup
    Reverse crotch lift
    Rear crotch lift
    Crotch lift
    Far crotch from standing behind
    Cross crotch lift
    Front crotch lift

Cross crotch lift

98. Crotch lift from rear standing
    Crotch lift when opponent stands
    High crotch lift
    Over crotch pickup
    Near crotch lift
    Crotch lift
    Rear crotch and body lift
    Outside crotch lift

Rear crotch lift

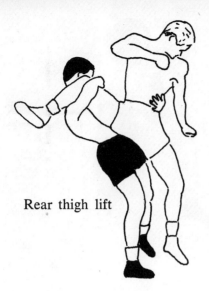

Rear thigh lift

99. Leg pickup from rear standing
Under thigh leg lift
Single leg lift to trip
Shoulder leg pick
Rear crotch lift
Rear knee lift
Knee lift
Near leg and body lift
Inside crotch lift
Rear leg lift

Grapevine counter
to rear thigh lift

100. Leg lever counter for crotch pickup
Bracing foot inside and opp. leg to prevent lift
Foot hook to block single leg lift
Foot in crotch—check for leg lift
Blocking rear crotch lift with leg
Hook leg as block for No. 99
Leg counter to knee lift
Inside leg hook or grapevine to counter lift
Toe block for outside crotch lift

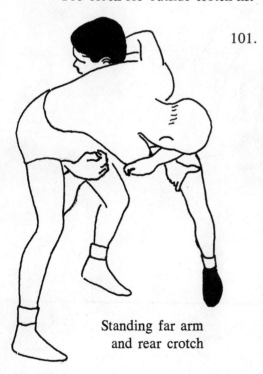

Standing far arm
and rear crotch

101. Far arm and outside crotch from
rear standing
Under arm sweep to cradle
Head under, cross arm and crotch drop
Head under arm spin
Far arm and rear crotch
Far arm and outside crotch

48

102. Single leg look and trip takedown
Over leg trip and inside opposite thigh lift
Back heel trip
Inside crotch, waist, and grapevine trip
Crotch lift with back heel (front)
Outside trip, inside lift
Set back
Near leg grapevine and inside far leg pickup
Waist and knee (standup block)
Standing navy ride

Inside crotch, waist
and grapevine trip

103. Hiplock throw with overhook and underhook
Over and under arm check
Hip throw (countering standup)
Over and under bar arm to reverse bar arm
1/2 nel & cross buttocks throw
Hiplock
Armlock and hip lift
Under arm hook to over arm bar & hiplock
Reverse hiplock

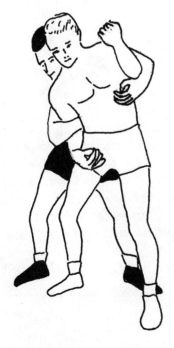
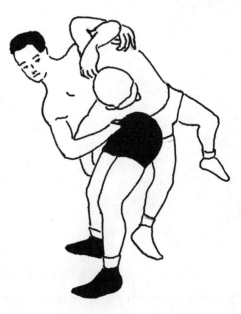

Hiplock throw with
bar arm and underhook

49

104. Hand pull release for No. 103
Under arm drag and finger pull
Counter for No. 103
Under cross arm reverse
Separating hands and standup
Arm drag counter for No. 103
Counter drag
Stand arm take hand away and turn in
Standing drag

Hand release for
hiplock throw

105. Pickup from rear standing
Waist lock and body lift
Body lift to counter standup break away
Rear lift
Taking to mat with rear body lock
Lift and put to mat from rear position
Body lift
Body hold and pickup
Rear bearhug lift
Reverse bear hug

Waist lock and lift

106. Leg grapevine counter
Locking (grapevining) to prevent lift
Hooking leg to prevent body lift
Leg grapevine block for rear lift
Reverse grapevine (to prevent lift)
Outside grapevine (counter for No. 105)
Grapevine counter to body lift
Outside grapevine (counter)
Grapevine block (for No. 105)

50

Grapevine counter
for waist lock and lift

107. Leg grab counter for rear standing
Thigh overhook when coming to stand
Countering grapevine ride
Outside crotch pickup
Grasp leg from outside
Outside leg pickup

Leg lift counter
for rear standing

Foot block
for leg pickup

108. Foot block for leg pickup
Countering grapevine ride
Reverse outside ankle pickup
Hook toe behind heel (counter No. 107)
Leg block to leg lift
Outside ankle pickup

109. Combination switch & roll
Standing step behind falling switch
Lateral reverse arm wing, sit through
Same as No. 62 (combination switch
and side roll)
Step behind heel
Winglock
Inside switch and roll combination
Standing roll and leg trip
Standing wing

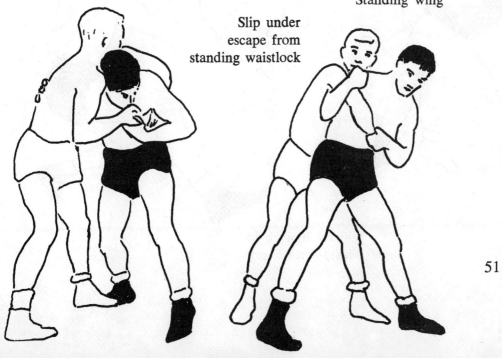

Slip under
escape from
standing waistlock

51

110. Whizzer hiplock counter for rear standing
Whizzer waistlock
Windmill hiplock (dropping the boom)
Whizzer to reverse crotch and cross arm
Overarm whizzer (windmill)
Double wing lock
Arm raise to hiplock position
Whizzer hip lock to inside crotch pry
Windmill into far arm & whizzer
Standing whizzer extended

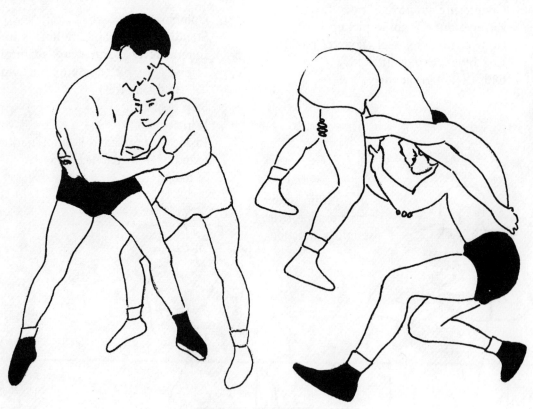

Whizzer hiplock to
inside crotch pry

111. Power crawfish
     Standing arm elevator
     Gizoni under arm movement
     Flying mare back out spinner
     Power sit out
     Spin under arm from front
     Under arm spin
     Standing sitout & underarm spin
     Power grab

Standing sit out
and underarm spin

Standing switch

112. Standing switch
Standing outside switch
Hip switch
Standing jump-out switch

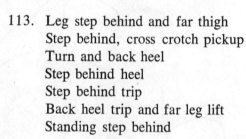

113. Leg step behind and far thigh
Step behind, cross crotch pickup
Turn and back heel
Step behind heel
Step behind trip
Back heel trip and far leg lift
Standing step behind

Step behind
cross thigh pickup

114. Cross face arm drag to ankle pickup
Shifting arm drag from front
Over head for arm bar and near leg pull
Cross arm drag to ankle pickup
Cross face bar arm and ankle
Arm drag with head in
Double arm drag and rear ankle
Near leg pry following cross arm tieup
Double arm drag & ankle
Tip

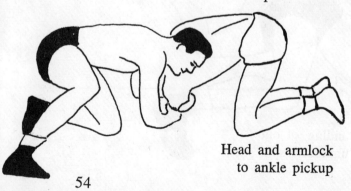

Head and armlock
to ankle pickup

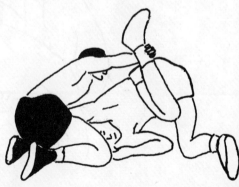

115. Arm drag from knees
Arm drag (face to face)
Double cross arm drag
Short arm drag
Double arm drag
Arm drag

Arm drag from knees

116. Head drag
Under arm sneak
Locked horns to head under arm
Slip under arm or head drag
Duck under

Head drag

117. Short arm drag
Elbow sweep
Short arm drag from knees
Back hand cross arm
Arm throw by
Drag by
Arm push or short arm drag
Elbow throw by
Arm push from knees

Elbow throw by

55

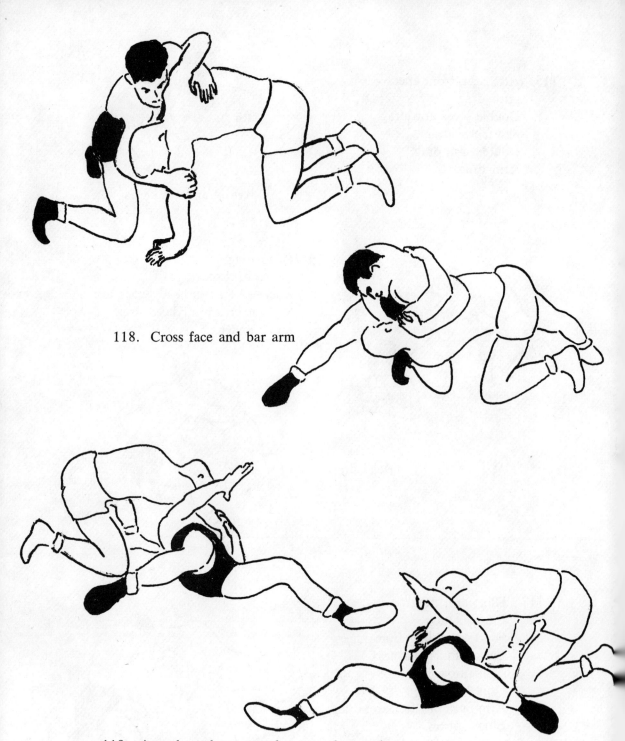

118.  Cross face and bar arm

119.  Arm through counter for cross face and
      bar arm

120. Head-on crotch pry

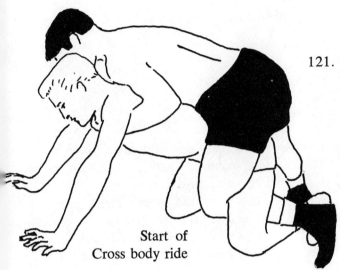

Start of
Cross body ride

121. Leg grapevine, start of cross body ride
Grapevining leg
Grapevine or cross body ride
High cross body ride
Cross body ride
Near leg hook or start of cross body scissor
Cross body ride
Near leg grapevine
Start of cross body ride
Near leg scissor breakdown
Cross body ride

122. Start of Guillotine
Cross ride with under arm hook
Starting Guillotine
Cross body ride flat
Cross body ride with modified hammerlock
Cross body scissor, opp. flat
Cross body with reverse arm
Cross scissor ride with under arm bar and wrist
Cross body ride with arm under (Guillotine start)
Drill
Cross body ride with arm hook

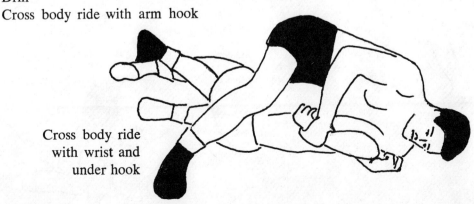

Cross body ride
with wrist and
under hook

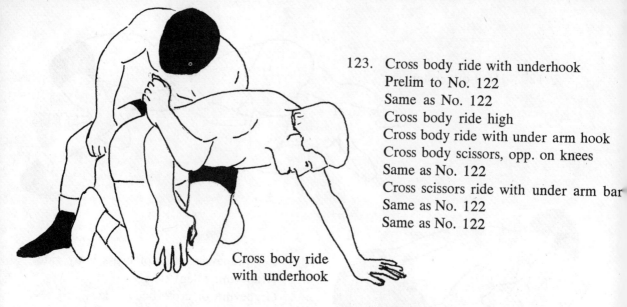

123. Cross body ride with underhook
Prelim to No. 122
Same as No. 122
Cross body ride high
Cross body ride with under arm hook
Cross body scissors, opp. on knees
Same as No. 122
Cross scissors ride with under arm bar
Same as No. 122
Same as No. 122

Cross body ride
with underhook

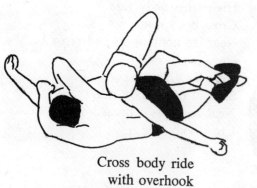

124. Cross body ride with over hook
Grapevine ride with double hook on leg
False pin, cross body ride
Cross body ride (immobilizing arm)
Cross body scissor, No. 122
Cross scissor ride with over arm hold
Cross ride

Cross body ride
with overhook

125. Buck counter for No. 124
Under arm and whizzer—trip lift
Escape from grapevine ride
Shake down of high body ride with
leg elevator
Leg block and elevator
Leg block and elevator
Shake off
Cross body ride
Shoulder slip
Elevator
Drill

Shake down escape
for cross body ride

126. Under arm whizzer and trip lift
Elevator escape
Counter with elevator
Leg block and elevator
Cross body ride
Far arm bár, near leg block and elevator
Elevator
Leg lift and roll

Counter for shakedown
escape using elevator and
leg block and pancake

127. Escape from grapevine
Lateral drift forming cross body
Drill off. Unhook leg & turn out or
    slip shoulder & turn in
Drill

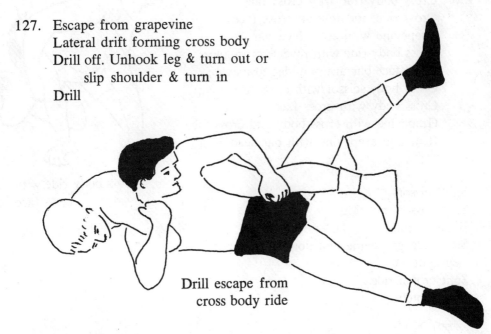

Drill escape from
cross body ride

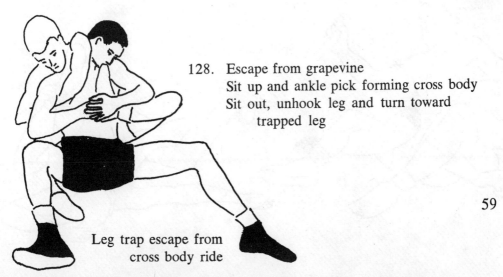

128. Escape from grapevine
Sit up and ankle pick forming cross body
Sit out, unhook leg and turn toward
    trapped leg

Leg trap escape from
cross body ride

59

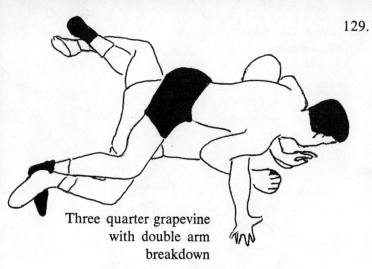

Three quarter grapevine
with double arm
breakdown

129. Three quarter stretcher
Three quarter grapevine ride
Grapevine ride with split double over
    head bar
Double arm and leg spread stretch
3/4 scissor
Double grapevine
Cross body with stretcher
Stretcher from leg grapevine, leg sprea
    and arm breakdown
Rear half grapevine with stretcher

130. Cross body ride with cross face
Cross ride and reverse cross face
Grapevine with cross face bar
Cross body ride with reverse cross face
Cross face bar arm with leg grapevine
Cross body scissor with cross face tieup
Cross body with cross face
Grapevine with cross body and cross face
Rear half grapevine with bar head

Cross body ride with
cross face

131. Split scissors
Split scissors position
Banana split
Single leg grapevine and double arm split
Leg split
Split crotch ride
Split crotch

Split scissors

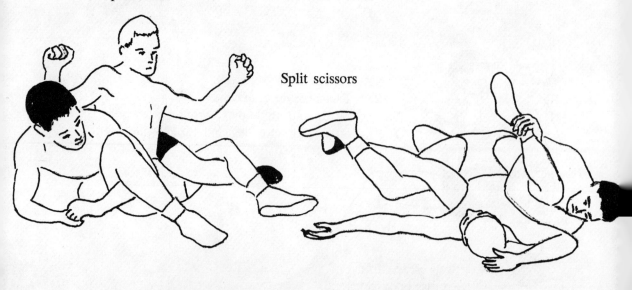

132. Figure four and arm knee hocklock split
Banana split arm pry combination

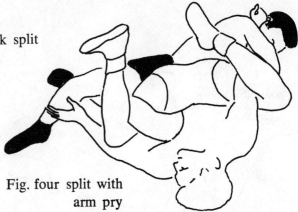

Fig. four split with
arm pry

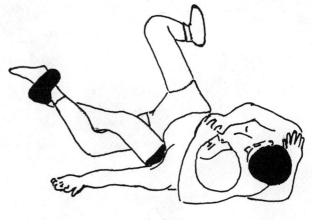

Leg grapevine with
reverse nelson cradle

133. Reverse nelson cradle with leg grapevine
Split scissors cradle
The country hold
Cradle and inside knee lock—spread split
Leg split with knee lock
Split crotch ride variation
Split crotch
Leg grapevine with reverse nelson cradle
Cradle

134. Guillotine
Crucifix
True cross body pin

Guillotine

135. Half nelson and cross ride grapevine
     Grapevine and half nelson
     False cross body pin
     Half nelson pin with cross body scissor
     Cross body and half nelson
     Near leg grapevine for half nelson
     Olympic fall back

Cross body
and half nelson

136. Tight waist and near arm pull breakdown
     Tight waist and near arm chop
     Breakdown
     Grapevine arm check
     Over bar on near arm
     Waist lock and near arm ride
     Near arm breakdown
     Waist and arm ride
     Near leg—near arm

Waist and arm
with overleg ride

137. Four point stand
     All fours position
     Grapevine leg trap
     Escape from overleg ride
     Stand up
     Leg hook and near arm pressure
     Near leg hook, body and near arm rid
     Halfstand

Escape from
overleg ride

138. Crotch pry and arm pull breakdown
Thigh lift and near elbow drive
Breakdown—destroying one of four supports
Near arm break down body drag
Driving opp. off balance with over bar arm
Break down by pulling
Crotch pickup and pressure near arm
Near arm and crotch pry
Waist and arm breakdown
Knee trip

Near arm and
crotch pry

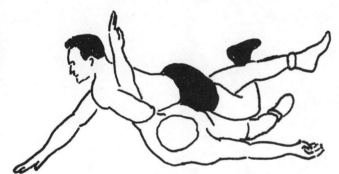

139. Reverse whizzer and grapevine

140. Two on one bar arm
Two on one (wrist) ride on far arm
Bar arm and waist lock
Double forearm ride
2 on 1 bar lock on far arm
Double bar arm ride
Further double bar arm
Double wrist chancery—far arm
Far double bar arm
2 on 1

2 on 1 far wrist

63

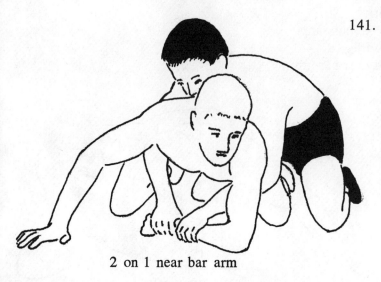

141. Two on one bar arm
2 on 1 ride on near arm
Bar arm and waist lock ride
Double forearm ride
2 on 1 barlock on near arm
Double bar arm ride
Near double bar arm
Double wrist chancery—near arm
Near double bar arm
2 on 1

2 on 1 near bar arm

142. Hand pry and twist release for 2 on 1
Finger pull release for 2 on 1
Freeing arm from 2 on 1—twist to thumb
Peel off
Pull hands loose
Take one hand off, straighten & twist
        right arm free
Double bar arm break

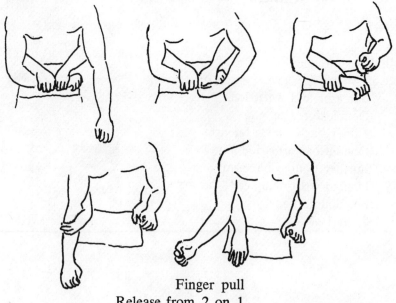

Finger pull
Release from 2 on 1

64

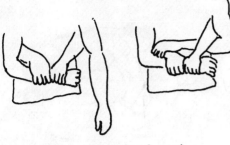
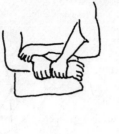

Arm pry
release from 2 on 1

143. Arm pry release for 2 on 1
Prying off 2 on 1
Swimmer's break for 2 on 1
Fireman's carry lift and slip break out
Working against thumb to break grip
Pry hands loose
Inter arm pry
Block far wrist, pry near arm up and
  twist both arms
Double bar arm break
Forearm lever

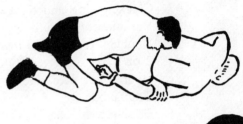

144. Under body bar
Bar arm and wrist pry
High bar and waist lock
Hammerlock & double bar arm trap
Arm lock and body press
Locked long waist lock ride
Arm lock
Bar hammerlock
The country pin
Wristlock

Waist bar hammerlock

145. 164 with body press position
Muscle pry with hammerlock
144 plus hammerlock ride
Body press
Counter for bar hammerlock—flatten out
The country pin

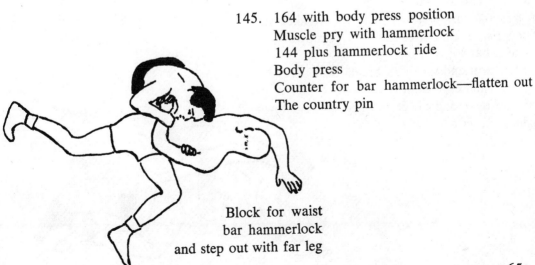

Block for waist
bar hammerlock
and step out with far leg

146. Bar arm and ankle block ride
    Leg in groin with body wt. pressure
    Bar arm and waist lock
    Leg block and forearm breakdown
    Near leg lock with 2 on 1 bar lock
    Double bar arm ride with knee up the back
    Near double bar
    Near leg and near arm breakdown
    2 on 1

Bar and foot
up the back

147. Chicken wing and tight waist breakdown
    Variation of 2 on 1
    Double forearm head lock trap
    2 on 1 bar lock variation
    Double bar arm ride variation
    Double bar
    Double wrist chancery

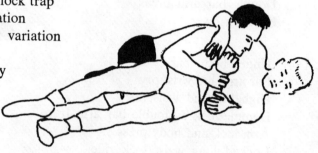

Variation of 2 on 1

148. Bar arm and crotch pry breakdown
    Near wrist and far thigh lift
    Bar arm and inside crotch lever for breakdown
    Inside wrist and far over crotch breakdown
    Near arm bar lock
    Near bar arm and far thigh breakdown
    Single bar and crotch lift
    Near arm tieup and far crotch pry to breakdown
    Single bar arm and lever (crotch)

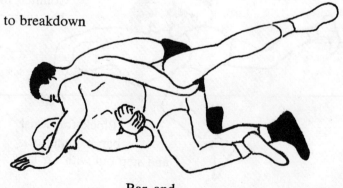

Bar and
crotch pry

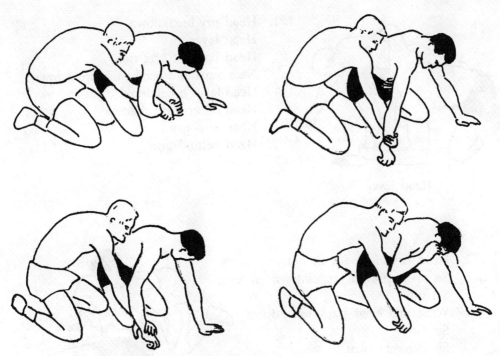

Releasing wrist hold

149. Release bar arm
    Releasing wrist hold
    Escaping bar arm—towards thumb
    Slip reverse from wrist ride
    Working against thumb
    Rotate wrist out of bar arm ride
    Arm twist
    Twist wrist to thumb
    Single bar arm break
    Straight arm

150. Chicken wing and crotch pry breakdown
    Bar hammerlock
    Chicken wing and waist lock
    Chicken wing and body drag breakdown
    Chicken wing and body drag breakdown
    Chicken wing and far thigh breakdown
    Near arm bar and far crotch pry to breakdown
    Winglock
    Arm hook

Chicken wing and
crotch pry

Head lever

151. Head pry breakdown
Head lever
Head back of arm ride
Near wrist and head back breakdown
Head lever breakdown
Head on arm breakdown
Near arm pry
Head behind arm

152. Head pry block for sit out
Sit up to prevent knockdown on lever
Set out
Wrist and head buck breakdown
Sit out
Sit out and turn
Near arm pry
Sit out to counter head lever
Sit away

Sit out counter
for head lever

153. Chicken wing and tight waist ride
Bar hammerlock
Chicken wing and waist lock
Chicken wing and body drag breakdown
Chicken wing
Winged hammerlock
Chicken wing and waist
Arm hook

Chicken wing

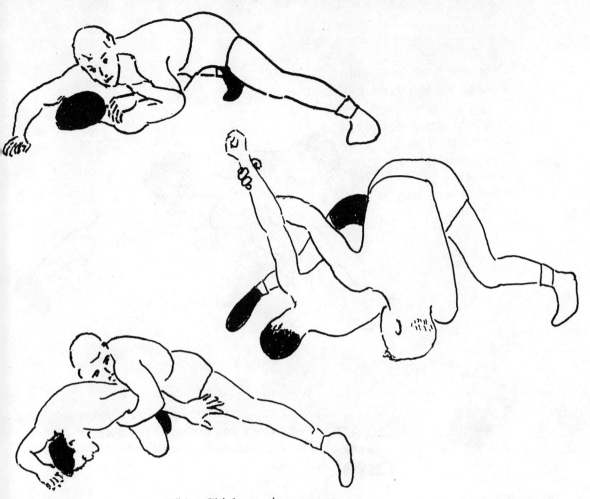

154. Chicken wing escape

155. Chicken wing and reverse arm bar
Bar hammerlock and bar arm
Double chicken wing
Chicken wing and bar arm
Chicken wing with near bar arm
Double hammerlock
Far chicken wing with near bar
Double bar arm

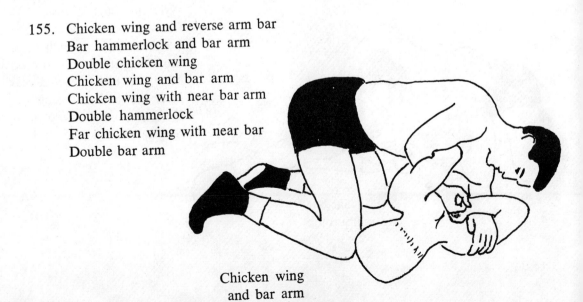

Chicken wing
and bar arm

156. Over arm hook breakdown
     Forcing bar hammerlock without head
     Diving chicken wing and waist lock
     Near bar arm and body
     Chicken wing, near side
     Chicken wing
     Near arm
     Chicken wing step behind
     Arm hook

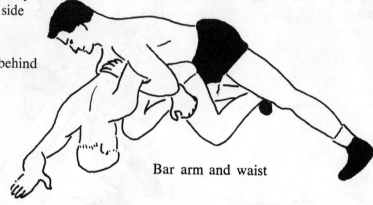

Bar arm and waist

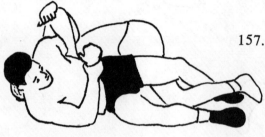

Wrist roll counter to
bar arm and waist

157. Wrist roll counter for chicken wing
     Wing and grapevine from bar hammerlock
     Wing down and under arm movement
     Hip roll and under lateral roll
     Outside roll
     Wing and drag
     Side roll to counter near arm bar
     Drag

158. Bar arm and outside crotch ride
     Wrist and outside crotch ride
     Bar arm and back crotch ride
     Wrist and over crotch breakdown
     Bar arm lock with rear crotch
     Near bar arm ride with rear crotch
     Near bar and rear crotch
     Near arm and rear crotch breakdown
     Single bar arm and crotch

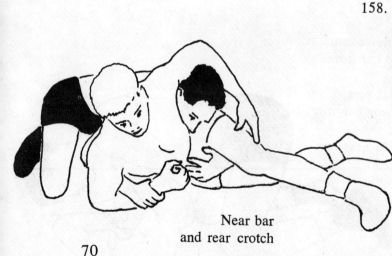

Near bar
and rear crotch

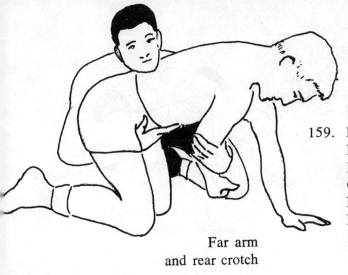

Far arm
and rear crotch

159. Far arm and outside crotch breakdown
Far arm and outside crotch
Back crotch and far arm bar
Cross arm and over crotch
Far arm bar with rear crotch
Far arm tieup and rear crotch
Far arm and rear crotch
Far arm and crotch

160. Bar arm stack up
High bar
Over crotch double arm
Bar arm lock from reach crotch
Locked long waist lock from rear
Rear crotch and double arm hold
Wrist chancery & arm hook after rear crotch
near arm breakdown
Crotch and double bar arm
2 on 1 through the crotch

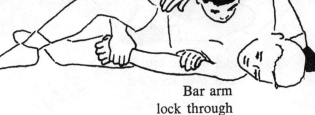

Bar arm
lock through
rear crotch

161. Bar arm and outside crotch
Near wrist and rear crotch thigh ride
Bar arm and back crotch
Wrist ride with over crotch to fall
Pin from locked long waist lock from rear
Bar arm and rear crotch
Near arm rear crotch to shoulder stand
Single bar arm & crotch
Stack

Near wrist rear crotch
to stack up

162. Near arm and outside crotch ride
Rear crotch and over shoulder ride
Back crotch and near arm breakdown
Over arm and over crotch ride
Stack up
Near arm hook and rear crotch
Rear crotch and over shoulder
Near arm and crotch
Near arm rear crotch

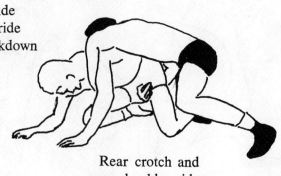

Rear crotch and
over shoulder ride

Counter to rear crotch
and over shoulder

163. Sit thru wrist roll to counter No. 162
Wrist grasps and roll to escape No. 162
Under arm and hip roll
Outside roll variation from No. 162
Rear wing and leg lift
Arm lock and roll counter (No. 162)

"Out the back door"

164. Kneelock elevator to counter No. 162
Escape through the back door
Roll under and leg lift
Under arm, near ankle with scissor kick
Pulling leg over head escape
Going out the back door
Leg pickup and roll out
Out the back door

72

165. Cross face and inside crotch breakdown
Cross face and back for leg breakdown
Cross arm with inside crotch
Far arm and rear crotch break down
Far leg and arm ride

Cross face
and inside crotch

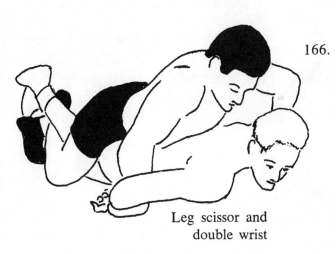

Leg scissor and
double wrist

166. Top leg scissor ride
Leg scissor and double wrist hold
Grapevine and double arm bar
Leg scissor top stretch
Double leg scissor
Double bar arm with leg scissor
Legs grapevined
Double arm breakdown and leg scissor ride
Near leg scissors stretch

167. Stretcher breakdown
Front stretch or riding scissors
Straight front scissor and double over head bar
Double leg and arms stretch
Top body scissors
Stretcher
Stretcher from top body scissors
Far leg grapevine stretcher
Body scissor and double grapevine

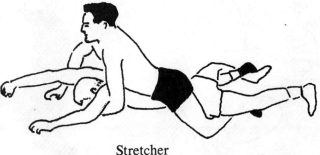

Stretcher

168.  Fig. 4 body scissors
Fig. 4 scissors
Fig. 4 scissors and double over head bar
Fig. 4 scissor with arm stretch
Fig. 4
Hook Scissor ride
Stretcher with fig. 4 scissor
Fig. 4 leg scissor

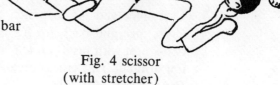

Fig. 4 scissor
(with stretcher)

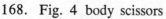

169.  Bridgeback, counter for fig. 4 body scissor
Backing opp. shoulders to mat
Best position to get opp. in if he has fig. 4
Arch back on fig. 4 scissors
Bridging into fig. 4 scissors
High bridge into hook scissor ride
Rare back
Arm lock and bridge to break 4 scissor
Bridge-back
Bridge back down

Bridgeback counter
for fig. 4 scissor

170.  Leg elevator counter for 4 scissor
Escape from 4 scissor
Ankle pickup and drift escape from 4 scissor
Breaking opponent's grapevine
Pull outside leg up and over head
Leg pickup to counter 4 scissor
Sit through and unhook legs to escape 4 scissor
Unhook it

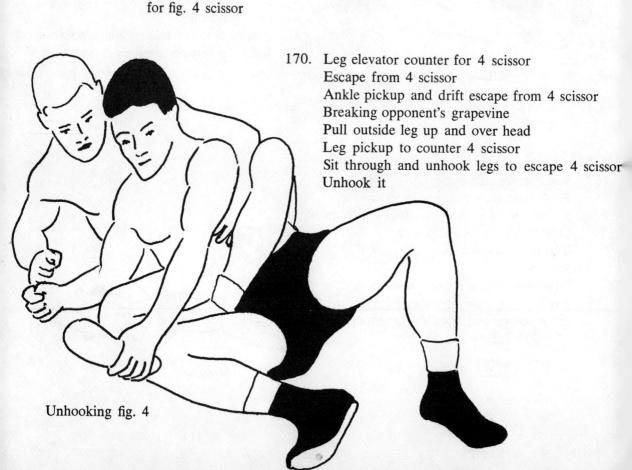

Unhooking fig. 4

171. Reverse nelson and fig. 4
Fall from fig. 4 with headlock combination
Fig. 4 with cross body pin
Fig. 4 with headlock
Hook scissor and headlock
Fig. 4 and headlock
Fig. 4 with leg hook and reverse nelson
Fig. 4 Guillotine

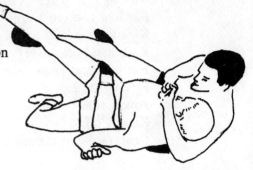

Fig. 4 with headlock

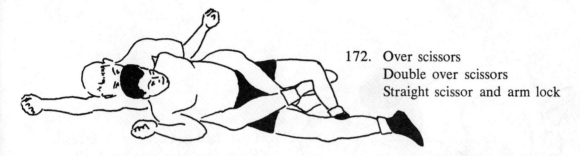

172. Over scissors
Double over scissors
Straight scissor and arm lock

Over scissor

173. Waist and far ankle breakdown
Under waist hook and far ankle
Waist lock and far ankle
Ankle ride
Far ankle ride
Far leg and waist hold
Waist and far ankle
Far ankle waist

Waist and
far ankle ride

174. Far arm and far ankle breakdown
Far arm and far ankle hold
Far ankle and cross arm
Far arm and far ankle ride
Far ankle and far arm

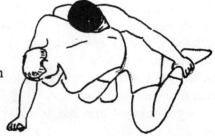

Far arm and far ankle

75

175. Kick off release for ankle breakdown
Kicking off hand grasp on far ankle
Far foot and cross arm
Kicking hand off to escape
Kick hand off ankle
Far foot and cross face
Freeing far leg
Ankle ride break
Kick it off
Cross face and far ankle

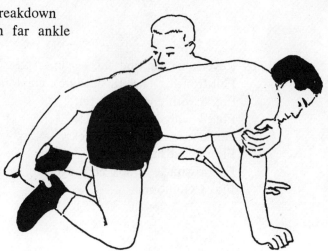

Kicking hand
loose from ankle ride

176. Cross face and near ankle breakdown
Cross face and near ankle lift
Near ankle and cross arm
Far arm and near ankle ride
Near ankle and cross face breakdown
Near ankle and cross face
Cross face and near ankle breakdown
Far arm & near ankle

Cross face
and near ankle

177. Chicken wing and ankle block ride
Bent leg in groin and barring near arm
Breakdown, Knee block and over bar arm
Near leg and near arm bar
Chicken wing with foot up the back
Groin ride and arm lock
Near leg block and arm bar breakdown

76

Bar arm and
foot up the back

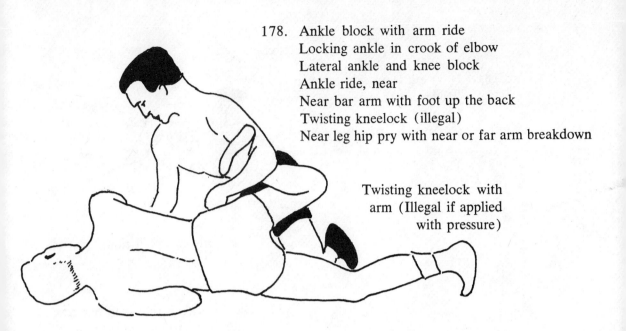

178. Ankle block with arm ride
Locking ankle in crook of elbow
Lateral ankle and knee block
Ankle ride, near
Near bar arm with foot up the back
Twisting kneelock (illegal)
Near leg hip pry with near or far arm breakdown

Twisting kneelock with
arm (Illegal if applied
with pressure)

179. Near ankle and waist breakdown
Near ankle lift from split leg in rear
Near ankle drive forward

Near ankle ride

180. Cross face and far ankle breakdown
Grasping fingers to prevent cross face
Far ankle and over near arm
Pull hand off cross face
Far ankle and cross face
Take hand away to counter cross face
Cross face break

Releasing cross face

181. Navy stack up ride position
Inside crotch ride
Lace ride
Cross crotch and body ride
Inside crotch and waist hold
The Oklahoma ride
Navy ride with waist

Inside crotch ride

Inside crotch ride
with wrist

182. Navy stack up ride with bar arm
Inside crotch ride and far wrist
Bar arm and lace ride
Cross crotch and wrist ride
Inside crotch ride with bar arm
Inside crotch and near wrist ride
Oklahoma ride with single bar
Navy ride with far wrist

183. Balanese trip
Thigh (leg) lift and step over far leg
Leg lift for step through
Near leg pickup
Near leg lift
Near leg lift and step through
Near leg pickup and step between
Near leg pickup and step over far leg
Leg lift and step through

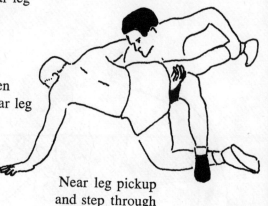

Near leg pickup
and step through

78

184. Balanese trip with 1/2 nelson
No. 162 with 1/2 nelson follow up
Step through with half nelson
Near leg pickup and cross step
Near leg lift with far leg grapevine
Near leg lift with step through and 1/2 nelson
Near leg pickup, step between and 1/2 nelson
Near leg pickup, step over far leg and
    long half nelson
Same as No. 183

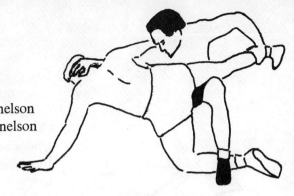

Step through
with half nelson

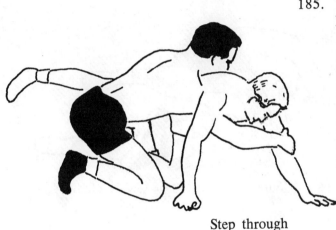

Step through
and far arm

185. Balanese trip with far arm
Far arm and far leg from underneath
Far leg and far arm breakdown
Far leg and under cross arm
Near leg and far arm breakdown
Near leg with step through and far arm
Step between and far arm
Far arm near leg breakdown
Leg lift and far arm
Far ankle, far arm

Near leg lift
and 1/2 nelson

186. Near leg and 1/2 nelson breakdown
1/2 nelson and near thigh lift
1/2 nelson and over crotch
1/2 nelson and rear crotch lift
Near leg lift and 1/2 nelson
Leg pickup and 1/2 nelson

79

187. Leg grapevine and stiff arm in crotch,
    counter 1/2 nelson
    Grapevine and drag—tailing out
    Countering 1/2 nelson
    Under arm with leg grapevine roll
    Blocking 1/2 nelson with near hand in crotch
    Counter 1/2 nelson with hand in crotch
    Inside switch with leg grapevine to counter
        1/2 nelson
    Run thru the 1/2, slip the 1/2

Grapevine & switch
counter for near
leg lift and
1/2 nelson

188. Counter for No. 187—scissor cradle

189. Pick hand off head counter for 1/2 nelson
    Taking off 1/2 by pulling fingers
    Countering 1/2 nelson
    Slipping 1/2 nelson
    Pulling 1/2 nelson off
    Pull hand off
    Take hand away
    Peel it off

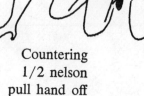

Countering
1/2 nelson
pull hand off

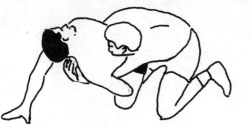

Counter 1/2 nelson
lock arm and
look away

190. Lock arm and look away block for 1/2
Winging arm that takes 1/2
Wingdown and head left to counter 1/2
Lateral wing to hip roll
Outside roll as def. for No. 186
Near wing and turn head away
Start of inside wing
Wing and stepover
Wing

191. Near side winglock
Winging arm that takes the 1/2
Dropping hip and raising head to counter 1/2
Wing and sit out
Sit out side roll
Winging 1/2 nelson
Near wing and sit out
Inside wing sit out or roll
Wing (block)
Wing

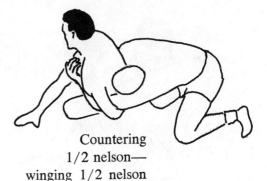

Countering
1/2 nelson—
winging 1/2 nelson

192. Block nearside 1/2 nelson with winglock
Winging arm that takes 1/2
Wing down 1/2 and step over
Lateral wing and step across
Near side roll
Near wing and cross over
Inside wing and step over
Wing and stepover
Wing

Counter 1/2—
wing and stepover

81

193. Slip 1/2 nelson
Stepping through to escape 1/2
Elbow wing sit through
Sliping a 1/2
Sit through No. 186
Near wing
Slip 1/2 & sit through
Under drag sit thru
Wing

Slipping the 1/2 nelson

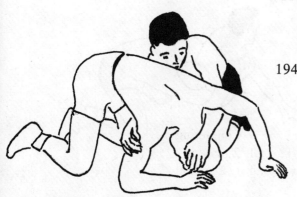

1/2 nelson
and far arm

194. 1/2 nelson and under far arm breakdown
1/2 nelson (near) and far arm (underneath)
1/2 nelson and barring 1/2
1/2 nelson with under cross arm
1/2 nelson with far arm lock
1/2 nelson and far arm

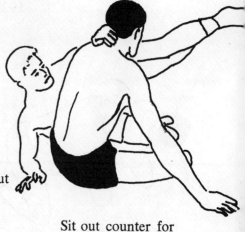

195. Sit out counter for 1/2 nelson
Dragging a 1/2 nelson—by tailing out
Near spin and leg lift
Inside switch to counter 1/2

Sit out counter for
1/2 nelson & far arm

82

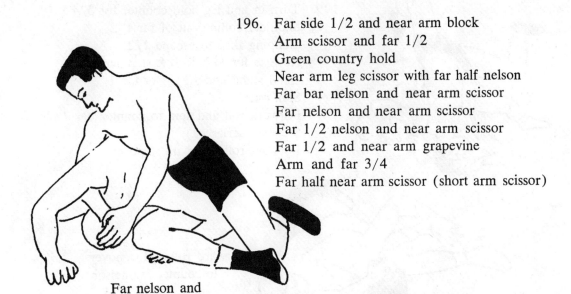

196. Far side 1/2 and near arm block
Arm scissor and far 1/2
Green country hold
Near arm leg scissor with far half nelson
Far bar nelson and near arm scissor
Far nelson and near arm scissor
Far 1/2 nelson and near arm scissor
Far 1/2 and near arm grapevine
Arm and far 3/4
Far half near arm scissor (short arm scissor)

Far nelson and
near arm scissor

197. Far side winglock
Winging 1/2
Hip roll wing
Side roll (locking elbow)
Outside roll far half nelson
Far wing
Outside winglock
Wing roll
Side roll

Counter far nelson
with wing

198. Slip 1/2
Dragging out of far 1/2
Stepping thru to escape 1/2
Far 1/2 nelson sit out
Sit through far 1/2
Under arm drag
Slip 1/2 nelson
Stepover series (1)
Run thru the 1/2 (slip the 1/2)

Slipping the far nelson

199. Turn in and leg hold counter for 3/4
Shoulder rolling out of far 1/2
Stepping thru to escape 1/2
Reverse for 1/2, Roll & step across
Head stand and step over far 1/2
Spin out
Forward roll and spin to counter bar 1/2
Stepover series (2)
Forward roll fake with stepover

Forward roll and stepover
to counter far nelson

200. 3/4 with leg hook
3/4 and near grapevine
3/4 nelson
3/4 with near leg straddle
Pullunder

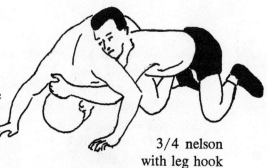

3/4 nelson
with leg hook

201. Double arm lock turn in (block 3/4)
Under winging 3/4
Tying arms and rolling to escape 3/4
Double wing and roll on 3/4
Winglock counter for 3/4
Outside roll 3/4
Lock arm counter to 3/4
Double elbow lock & roll to counter 3/4
Pullover break

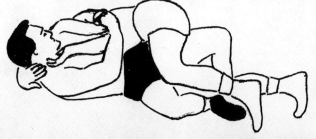

Double arm lock
counter for 3/4

202. Sit out counter for 3/4
   Sitting to prevent 3/4
   Escape from 3/4
   Double wing on 3/4 and sit out
   Lock hands and sit out (block 3/4)
   Set out counter to 3/4
   Double elbow lock and sit out

Sit out counter
   for 3/4

203. Turn in and leg hold counter for 3/4
   Blocking straight 3/4 with leg grab
   Countering 3/4
   Inside crotch switch on 3/4
   Grasp ankle from inside as block for 3/4
   Sit out and inside switch
   Pullunder block

Turn in and leg
counter for 3/4

204. 1/2 nelson and inside crotch
   1/2 nelson and crotch to fall
   1/2 nelson and crotch fall hold
   1/2 nelson and crotch lift pin
   Inside crotch & 1/2 nelson
   1/2 nelson and crotch

1/2 nelson and crotch

205. Bridge & turn in counter for
       1/2 nelson & crotch
     Slipping arm to turn from back on
       1/2 and crotch
     Slipping arm thru to escape 1/2
     Creep-in roll
     Escape from inside crotch & 1/2
     Bridge high and turn in
     Bridge up
     Bridge, drive outside arm thru and turn in
     1/2 nelson and crotch break (uphill)
     Bridge & turn in

Bridge and turn in
counter for crotch & 1/2

206. 1/2 nelson with farther wrist
     1/2 nelson and body press
     Block 205 by grasping far arm
     1/2 nelson and far arm
     1/2 nelson, wrist hold and body press
     1/2 nelson & far wrist

To stop bridge and
turn in take
1/2 nelson and far wrist

Rolling counter for
crotch & 1/2 nelson

207. Roll over counter for crotch & 1/2
     Grasping leg to get parallel and roll man
     Escape from 1/2 nelson and crotch
     Double arm in crotch turn
     Lock hands in No. 204, complete def. with roll
     Lock arms around leg and roll out
     Leg lock to counter 1/2 nelson

86

Modified 3/4 nelson

208. Partial 3/4 nelson
3/4 nelson and leg lock
3/4 nelson
Over 3/4 nelson
Modified 3/4 nelson
3/4 nelson with arm inside
1/4 nelson pullunder
False nelson

209. Elbow lock and lunge block for 3/4
Sprawling to prevent 3/4
Sprawling to counter 3/4
Stretching block for 3/4
Force head up as block for No. 208
Flatten out block to 3/4
Drop shoulder & turn away
1/4 nelson block

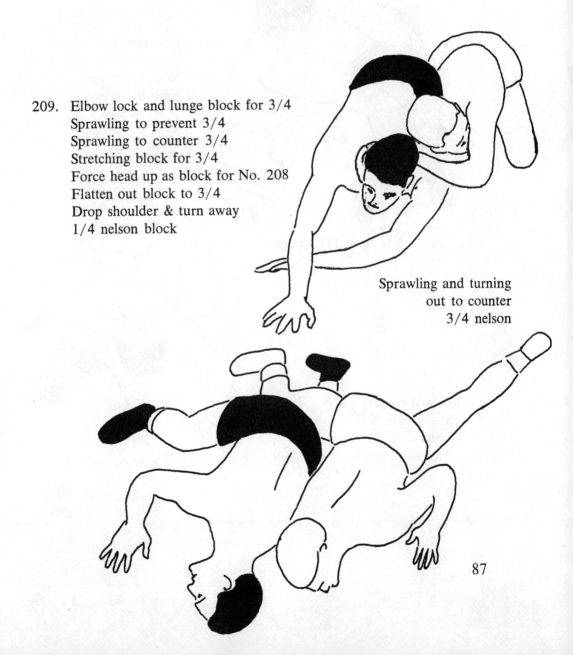

Sprawling and turning
out to counter
3/4 nelson

87

210. Flatten out block for 3/4
Flatten out
Sprawling
Countering modified 3/4
Force head up as block
Flatten out, head up, widen base

Flattening out to block
3/4 nelson

211. Extended 1/2 nelson
Forced 1/2 nelson
Near 1/4 nelson
Near bar nelson

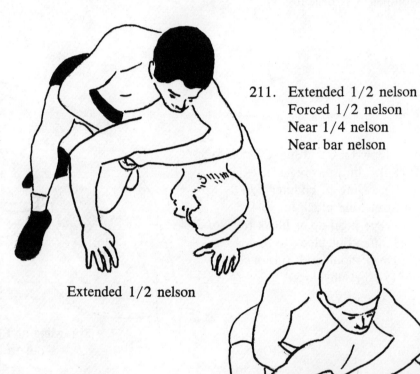

Extended 1/2 nelson

212. Turn in leg hold counter for No. 211
Turn in to block No. 211
Set out counter to 1/4 nelson
Sit out and inside switch to counter No. 176

Leg counter for
extended 1/2 nelson

1/4 nelson

213. 1/4 nelson
Near bar 1/2 nelson
Barred nelson pullunder

214. Stepover block for 1/4 nelson
Stepover
Stepover on near bar 1/2 nelson
Drop head to mat and step over

Stepover counter
for 1/4 nelson

215. Sit thru arm lock (counter No. 213)
Back wing
Double arm tie up set through
Sit through under
Reverse winglock—variation
Set through
Take hand off neck, reverse wing and
sit through
Head-to-head roll
Tip

Sit through arm lock
counter for 1/4

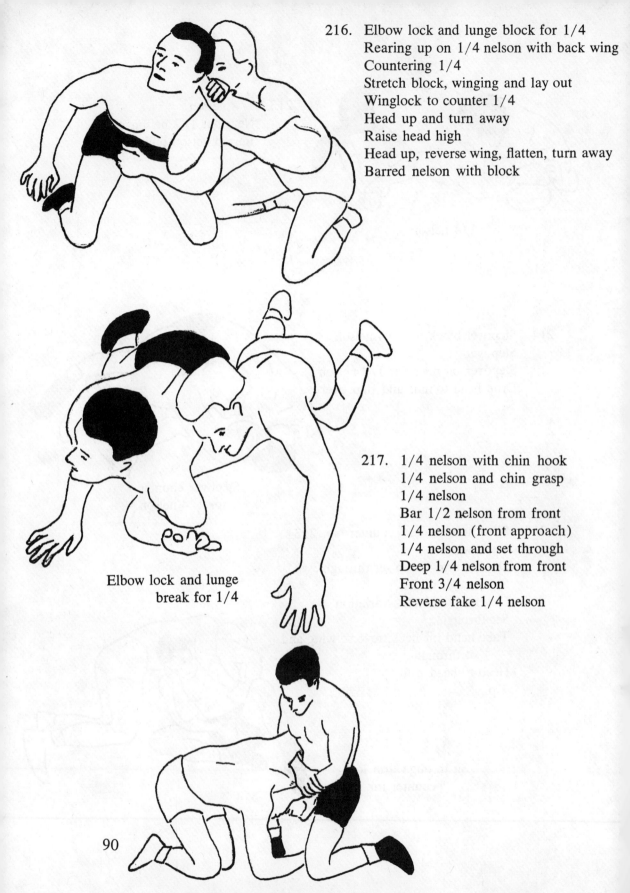

216. Elbow lock and lunge block for 1/4
Rearing up on 1/4 nelson with back wing
Countering 1/4
Stretch block, winging and lay out
Winglock to counter 1/4
Head up and turn away
Raise head high
Head up, reverse wing, flatten, turn away
Barred nelson with block

217. 1/4 nelson with chin hook
1/4 nelson and chin grasp
1/4 nelson
Bar 1/2 nelson from front
1/4 nelson (front approach)
1/4 nelson and set through
Deep 1/4 nelson from front
Front 3/4 nelson
Reverse fake 1/4 nelson

Elbow lock and lunge
break for 1/4

1/4 nelson with chin

218. Extended far half nelson
Far 1/2 nelson with near arm extension
Forced 1/2 nelson
Bar 1/2 nelson from rear
Bar nelson, far side
Forced far half nelson
Far 1/4 nelson
Far bar nelson
Barred nelson
Cross body

Extended far nelson

Chicken wing and
1/2 nelson

219. Arm bar and near 1/2 nelson
Chicken wing and 1/2 nelson
1/2 nelson with chicken wing
1/2 nelson and far wing
1/2 nelson and bar arm

220. Roll to counter chicken wing and 1/2 nelson
Wing and drag from No. 219
Set through to counter No. 219
Roll under
Side roll to counter No. 219
Outside roll chicken wing arm
Slip 1/2 nelson and side roll
1/2 nelson and wing break (roll)
High wing

Roll counter to
chicken wing and 1/2

221. Drag to counter chicken wing
Back dragging
Countering chicken wing
Brace and raise chicken wing
Straightening arm—counter chicken wing
Stand up in chicken wing
Stand up counter
Windmill break for wing

Drag to counter
chicken wing

Reverse nelson
and wrist

222. Reverse nelson & reverse bar arm
Rev. 1/2 nelson and wrist
1/4 nelson
Reverse front 1/2 nelson
Front 1/2 nelson and bar
Front 1/4 nelson & bar arm
1/4 nelson wrist chancery
Front reverse nelson and bar arm
Reverse 1/2 nelson

223. 1/4 nelson
Reverse bar front 1/2 nelson
Reverse 1/4 nelson
Front 1/4 nelson
Front 3/4 nelson
Rev. 1/4 nelson

Front 1/4 nelson

224. Leg nelson
    Reverse front leg 1/2 nelson
    Leg 1/2 nelson
    1/4 nelson with leg
    Front leg nelson

Leg nelson

225. Reverse nelson & inside crotch
    Crotch and under neck
    Under 1/2 nelson, crotch and body press
    Reverse nelson & crotch

Reverse nelson
and crotch

226. Cuddle bridge and turn out escape from 225
    Bridging & slipping arm through
        between bodies
    Turn in, chin push and turn away
    Bridge & turn in, drive chin, slip inside
        arm thru and turn away
    Bridge and roll away

Bridge & turn out
    to escape
Reverse nelson
    & crotch

93

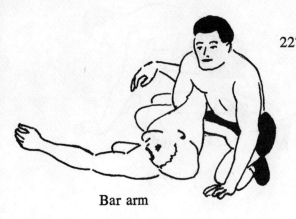

Bar arm

227. Over arm lock ride
Bar arm
Arm grapevine
Over arm hook
Chicken wing bar above elbow
Reverse arm lock
Arm bar
Single arm control

228. Arm hook
Under arm check & cross face
Bar arm
Reverse arm hook
Under arm hook
Under arm jerk back
Reverse arm bar and chin hold
Single arm approach

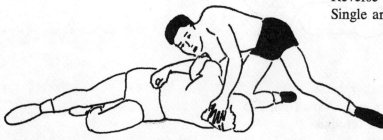

Arm hook and
face counter

229. Head chancery and waist lock
1/2 nelson & deep waist lock
Bar arm and 1/2 nelson
Deep 1/2 nelson & body
1/2 nelson & body chancery
1/2 nelson & body lock
Double double
1/2 nelson body hold
1/2 nelson & waist
1/2 nelson & body
1/2 nelson & body press

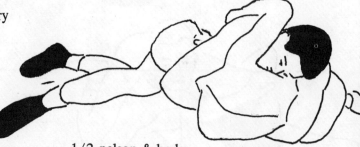

1/2 nelson & body

94

230. Top body scissor & 1/2 nelson
Rev. double leg scissor & arm
Straight front scissor, half nelson and bar
Double leg stretcher with deep 1/2 nelson
Top body scissor with 1/2 nelson
Top scissor & half nelson
Reverse stretcher
Top body scissor, half nelson & arm lock
1/2 nelson & under arm hook with scissors
1/2 nelson & leg scissors

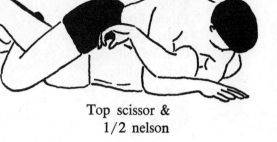

Top scissor &
1/2 nelson

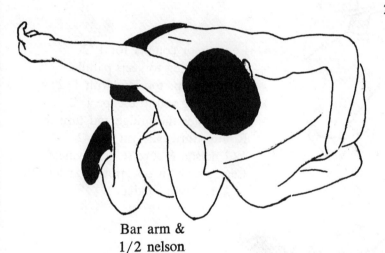

Bar arm &
1/2 nelson

231. Bar arm & 1/2 nelson
1/2 nelson & far wrist
1/2 nelson & single bar arm
1/2 nelson & body

232. Sit out counter for bar & 1/2 nelson
Raising body to prevent nelson
Set through to counter bar & 1/2 nelson
Wrist drag & sit out
1/2 nelson and bar arm counter
Sit thru bar arm & 1/2
Set out counter to 1/2
Standup or sit out to counter 1/2 nelson
     bar arm
1/2 nelson single bar arm break
Sit thru

Sit out counter
for bar & 1/2 nelson

233. Near side roll counter for bar & 1/2
     Wing & arm lift
     Elbow lift and set through
     Wrist drag & sit out roll
     Outside roll
     Drag counter
     Side roll
     Sit thru drag
     Slip the 1/2

Arm roll to counter
bar & 1/2 nelson

234. Leg scissor counter for 1/2
     Scissoring leg to keep parallel
     Getting opp. too low with 1/2 &
     completing roll to escape 1/2
     Roll under the bridge and turn in
     Rolling thru bar arm & 1/2
     1/2 nelson & reverse grapevine
     Leg scissor, sit up, stretch far leg and
        roll opp. under

Leg scissor block
for bar & 1/2

235. Hammerlock & 1/2 nelson
     Back bar & 1/2
     Deep 1/2 nelson with hammerlo
     Wrist & 1/2
     1/2 nelson & reverse bar
     1/2 & wristlock

Hammerlock &
1/2 nelson

236. Fig. 4 body scissor & 1/2
     Fig. 4 & near 1/2
     Fig. 4 & 1/2
     Fig. 4 & 1/2 nelson twister
     Hook scissor & 1/2
     1/2 & hook scissor

Fig. 4 scissor &
1/2 nelson

237. Reverse nelson cradle
     Far cradle
     Cradle
     Far cradle
     Jack knife cradle
     Cross cradle from reverse 1/2 nelson
     Roll back cradle
     Reverse cradle

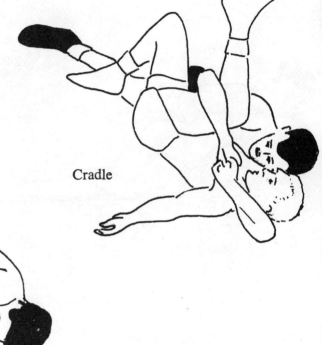

Cradle

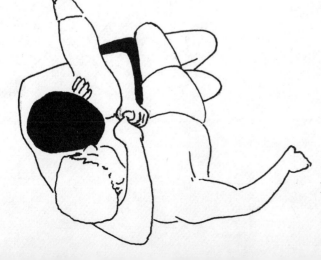

238. Reverse nelson with near leg cradle
     Near cradle
     Cradle
     Reverse cradle
     Near leg cradle put on backwards
     Near leg cradle
     Rolling cradle
     High cradle

97

Reverse cradle
with near leg

Cradle with
Grapevine

239. Reverse nelson cradle with leg grapevine
    Far cradle and grapevine
    Cradle with leg hook
    Far cradle with near leg block
    Far leg cradle
    Cross cradle from reverse half nelson
        with leg scissor
    Roll-back cradle & barred leg
    High cradle & leg
    Reverse cradle & leg lock

Cradle with
reverse leg hold

240. Reverse nelson with outside far leg cradle
    Far cradle & leg cover
    Cradle without side hook
    Far knee brace cradle with step-in
    Cradle variation
    Cross cradle with leg hooked backwards
    Cradle with reverse leg grip
    Rev. nelson cradle & near leg block,
        locking leg from outside
    Varied roll-back cradle

241. Crotch & arm hold
    Far arm & cross crotch pickup
    Cradle variation
    Arm & leg tie up in cradle position
    Inside crotch & arm hold
    Jack knife and arm lock
    Stacking cradle

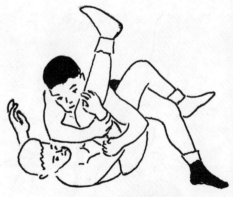

Cradle variation

Reverse cradle with
far leg

242. 1/2 nelson cradle
Forcing near cradle to fall
Cradle without side hook
Far cradle with body press
Near side cradle
Near leg cradle from 1/2 nelson
Cradle
1/2 nelson cradle
Side cradle
1/2 nelson & far leg
Cradle with far leg

243. Sit thru counter for 1/2 nelson cradle
Sitting thru to escape cradle
Set thru to counter cradle
Getting arm inside cradle
Sit through counter
Side cradle block

Sit through counter
for reverse cradle
with far leg

244. Leg grab counter for near leg cradle
    Grasping inside leg to counter
    Leg pull counter
    Turn in to ankle drag
    Turning in cradle
    Counter to cradle
    Drive inside arm thru and lock opp.'s leg

Leg counter for
reverse cradle

245. Far arm grapevine and inside crotch
    Inside crotch and armlock
    Crotch & arm bar
    Arm grapevine with crotch lift
    Arm lock and crotch
    Chicken wing bar above elbow and crotch
    Crotch & reverse arm lock
    Turkey bar and inside crotch
    Body press (wing & crotch)

Far arm grapevine
with front crotch

246. Bar arm position
    Bar arm, double arm bar
    Arm grapevine check, far arm jaw brace bar
    Arm lock & double arm tieup
    Chicken wing bar above elbow and arm tieup
    Reverse arm lock
    Arm bar and far arm lock
    Double arm pin
    Single bar arm

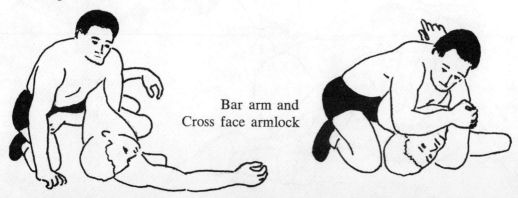

Bar arm and
Cross face armlock

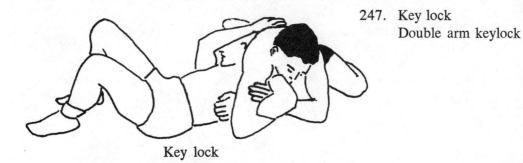

247. Key lock
Double arm keylock

Key lock

248. Reverse nelson strait jacket-rev. double bar
Double bar arm
Upside down double-double
Double reverse bar arm
Double bar lock
Reverse 1/2 nelson & locked bar under back
Reverse double double
Reverse double bar
Double-double
Double arm bar

Reverse double
bar lock

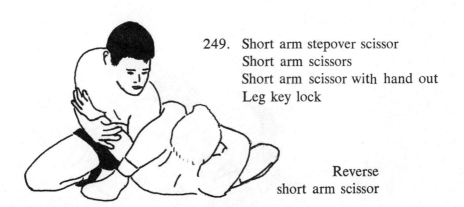

249. Short arm stepover scissor
Short arm scissors
Short arm scissor with hand out
Leg key lock

Reverse
short arm scissor

250. Short arm scissor
Sort of short arm scissor
Leg keylock
Short arm fig. 4 scissor
Fig. 4 keylock

Short arm scissor

Rolling escape from
short arm scissor

251. Roll over escape from No. 250
Coming to knees escape
Back rolling out of No. 250
Short arm scissor
Fig. 4 keylock break

252. Reverse double bar
Double bar arm
Over head double bar arm
Near bar arm with 1/2 nelson stretcher
Double arm tieup back of neck
Double arm lock
Reverse double-double

Double arm bar

253. Double bar nelson
Rev. double bar arm
Over head double arm bar
1/2 nelson with double stretcher
Reverse double bar nelson
Locked double arm tieup back of neck
Princeton
Reverse double bar
Princeton bar
Double bar arm

Overhead double
arm bar

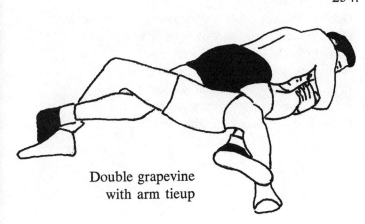

Double grapevine
with arm tieup

254. Double grapevine with arm tieup
Rev. double grapevine
Start front scissors with over head
double arm bar
Spread eagle with double arm stretcher
Top body scissors
Double grapevine & double arm tieup
Reverse stretcher
Top body double grapevine with both
arms and head
Double arm bar with double grapevine
Spread eagle
Double leg grapevine

255. Reverse double wristlock
Japanese wristlock with body press
Reverse wristlock
Barred reverse hammerlock

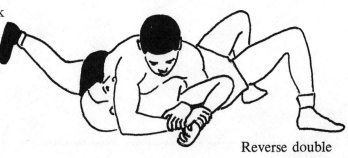

Reverse double
wristlock

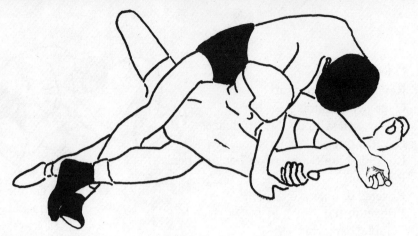

Overhead double
bar arm and
body scissor

256. Stretcher to double bar nelson (Princeton)
Double bar arm and str. body scissor
Body scissors with over head double arm bar
Straight body scissor with double
arm stretcher
Double bar nelson & body scissors
Double arm tieup and straight scissor
Straight body scissor and Princeton
Body scissor and double bar lock
Princeton bar with closed scissor
Double bar arm & body scissors
Cross body scissor & double arm bar

257. Start of Princeton
Barring both arms with one
Moving into No. 256
Fig. 4 with double bar arm stretcher
Double bar nelson and body scissor (var.)
Double arm tieup and hook scissor
Fig. 4 & Princeton
Fig. 4 body scissor with double bar lock
Princeton bar with open scissor

Overhead double
bar arm
with 4 scissor

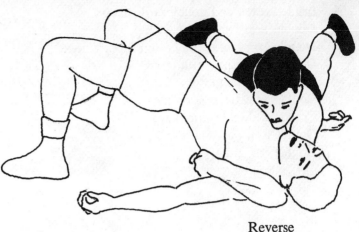

258. Reverse nelson strait jacket
    Arm bar and body lock
    Upside down double-double
    Under 3/4 nelson
    Double bar lock
    Reverse half nelson and locked bar under back
    Reverse double-double
    Reverse double wristlock
    Barred reverse nelson
    Double-double

Reverse
double barlock

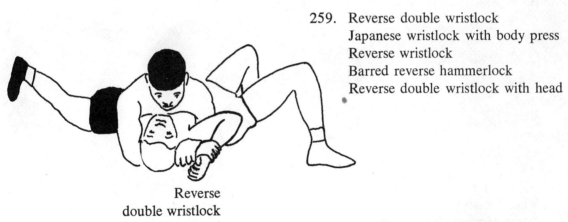

259. Reverse double wristlock
    Japanese wristlock with body press
    Reverse wristlock
    Barred reverse hammerlock
    Reverse double wristlock with head

Reverse
double wristlock
behind head

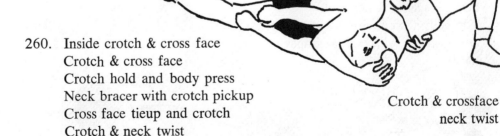

260. Inside crotch & cross face
    Crotch & cross face
    Crotch hold and body press
    Neck bracer with crotch pickup
    Cross face tieup and crotch
    Crotch & neck twist
    Crotch hold and head hold

Crotch & crossface
neck twist

261. Inside crotch and double arm tieup
Double arm lock and crotch
Double arm tieup with crotch & body press
Double cross arm with crotch
Double arm tieup
Double arm tieup & crotch
Crotch & double arm tieup
Double arm pin & crotch
Double bar arm

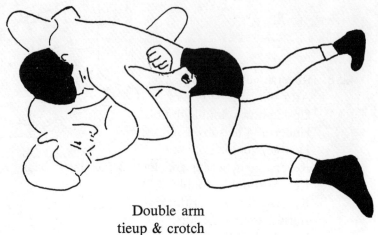

Double arm
tieup & crotch

262. Half nelson & crotch hold with body press
Reverse neck bracer with crotch
Body press

Crotch & neck twist
(arm caught
across chest)

263. Straight body scissor with knee lock
Knee lock from scissor
Body scissor with leg hook
Straight body scissor with double knee lock
Knee lock
Straight open scissor hooked on the far leg
Straight scissor & leg hook
Top body with double grapevine on far leg
Open scissor with double grapevine

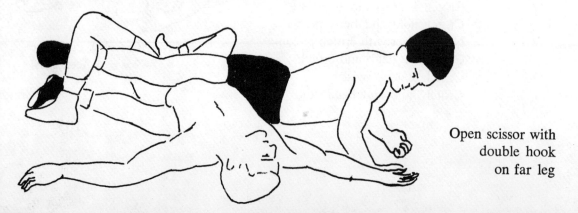

Open scissor with
double hook
on far leg

264. Crab ride with 2 on 1 bar
2 on 1 & crab ride
Bar arm and leg elevators
Under stretcher ride
Crab ride
Double arm ride with outside leg hooks
Double bar arm and leg spread
Double wrist chancery & body hold with
inside leg hooks
Double barred arm with elevator
2 on 1 sit behind

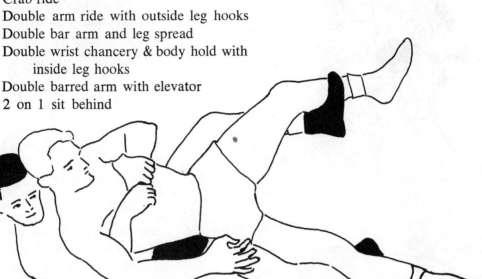

Crab ride with
2 on 1 bar

265. Sit down counter for crab ride
Break for crab ride
Escape from No. 264
Brace on leg—lateral drift
Crab ride escape
Backing into No. 264 as defense
Scoot out counter to No. 264
Shift legs and body to perpendicular to
reverse opp.
Elevator block

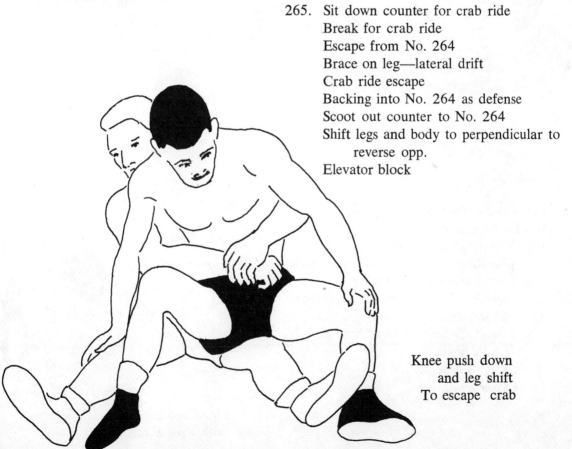

Knee push down
and leg shift
To escape crab

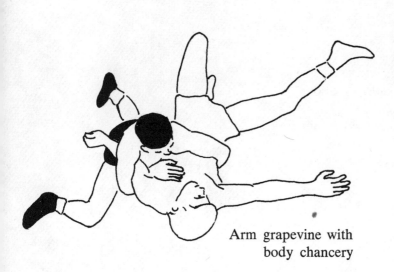

266. Arm grapevine & body lock
     Waist lock & arm bar
     Arm grapevine with body press
     Arm lock and body chancery
     Arm tieup and body chancery
     Single whizzer
     Turkey bar with body hold
     Wing & waist (front)
     Single bar with body lock

Arm grapevine with
body chancery

267. Bar arm & fig. 4 head scissor
     Head scissor & arm
     Fig. 4 scissor on head and arm bar
     Fig. 4 head scissor
     Fig. 4 head scissor with ankle
     Hook scissor on head with far arm
     Head scissor with arm & arm lock

Fig. 4 head scissor
and arm bar

268. Fig. 4 head scissor with leg hook
     Head scissor & leg
     Fig. 4 scissors bar on forearm & leg
     Fig. 4 head scissors with lateral knee lock
     Fig. 4 head scissors with ankle
     Hook scissors on head with far leg and arm
     Head scissor with ankle hold
     Fig. 4 head scissor with wrist hold &
         outside ankle pry
     Varied fig. 4 head scissor
     Head scissor with leg

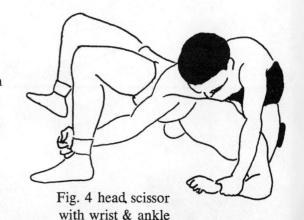

Fig. 4 head scissor
with wrist & ankle

269. Roll over escape from fig. 4 head scissor
Turning or spinning from head scissors
Head scissor to escape fig. 4 on head
Roll & step over
Fig. 4 scissor escape by bridge
Bridging & turning as def., against 220
Bridge & turn in

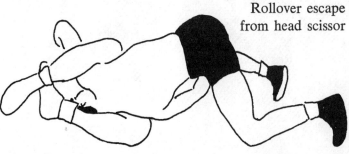

Rollover escape
from head scissor

270. Short switch
Prelim hand removal in prep for switch
True switch
Outside switch
Knock hand off arm & switch
Pivot switch
Tight switch

Outside switch

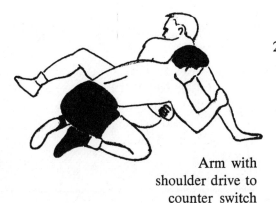

Arm with
shoulder drive to
counter switch

271. Arm pull block for switch
Checking a switch with arm and waist drive
Shoulder drive to counter switch
Far arm block for switch
Re-switch
Holding arm
Arm tieup to counter switch
Near arm break (counter switch)
Crowding switch block
Suck him in

109

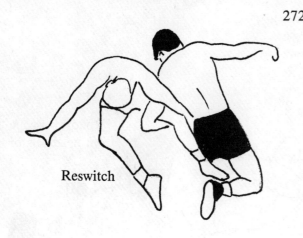

272. Inside leg reswitch
Dropping to thigh and following
Set thru reswitch
Counter switch
Reswitch
Sitout block for switch

Reswitch

273. Stepover counter for switch
Jumping across man to stop switch
Stepping over switch
Switch block stepover
Stepover
Start of crossover on switch

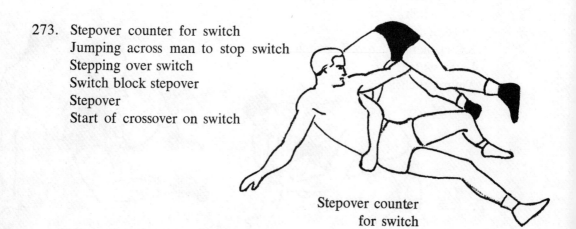

Stepover counter
for switch

274. Extended switch or leg switch
Leg switch
Power switch
Elongated switch
Leg extension switch
Extension switch
Extended switch

Extended switch

Outside wing
and elevate

275. Wing & leg lift
Wing & leg lift
Wing or roll
Hip roll with leg elevator
Side roll with inside leg elevator
Outside roll
Winglock
Outside side roll
Side roll
Far wing

276. Flatten out
Sprawling
Leg straddle drift back block
Side roll counter
Drop wt. back on near side
Flatten out
Power block
Sprawl
Drag back

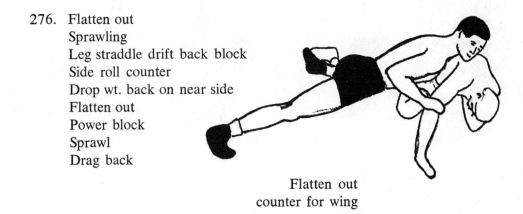

Flatten out
counter for wing

Grapevine counter
for wing

277. Cross body block for roll
Grapevine counter for wing
Go with roll, counter with grapevine
Slipping into cross body ride
Cross body block for roll
Rolling into cross body scissor
Single scissor and roll through
Arm & scissor block
Scissor leg

Sit out turn in

278. Sit out turn in
     Forward sitout & turn in
     Setting out in front
     Sit out and turn
     Sit out
     Set out
     Front sit out

279. Head pry block for sit out
     Head lever on arm & waist
     Head back of arm ride to stop set out roll
     Body drag with arm buck
     Head lever
     Pulling back to prevent sit out
     Arm lever
     Head lever
     Head behind arm

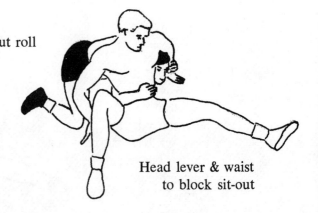

Head lever & waist
to block sit-out

280. Over arm drag (counter for sit out & turn in)
     Circling head on sit out
     Arm pull to go around and meet set out & roll
     Reverse arm hook & floating switch
     Reverse drag
     Dragging and moving towards sit out
     Hook arm, over drag
     Under arm bar, drop, drag near arm and
         spin behind
     Pull back
     Over drag

Over arm drag
counter for sit out
and turn in

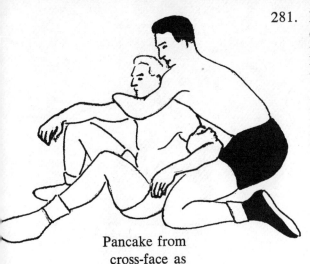

281. Pancake from cross face position
    Cross arm check & throw back
    Blocking set out
    Reverse arm hook, cross arm, arm grapevine
        cross arm drag back
    Reverse arm bar
    Jerk back
    Lateral drop
    Near under arm bar to far arm & drop back
    Drag & pull back

Pancake from
cross-face as
counter for sit out

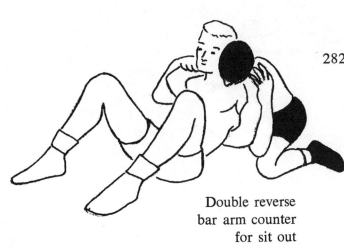

282. Arm lock counter for sit out
    Over checking arms on sit out
    Over arm lock
    Over double arm bar drag back
    Snap back
    Jerk back into reverse 1/2 nelson &
        locked bar under back
    Reverse double double
    Double over arm bar drop back
    Over arm bar
    In front of both arms

Double reverse
bar arm counter
for sit out

283. Arm & chin hook counter
    Back arm & chin grasp
    Jerk back
    Over & under double drag back
    Snap back
    Reverse double double
    Over arm bar & chin drop back
    Arm & chin pull back

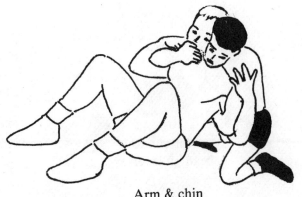

Arm & chin
counter for
sit out

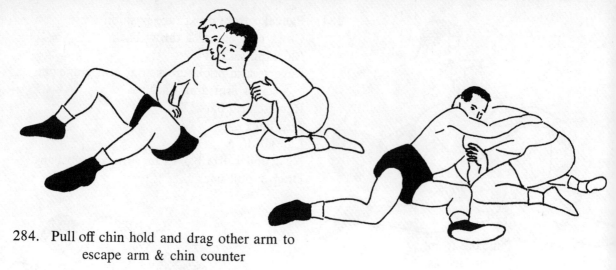

284. Pull off chin hold and drag other arm to
    escape arm & chin counter

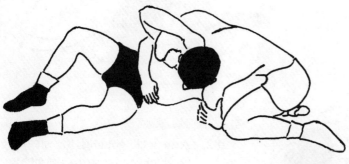

285. Lock head over shoulder and elbow to
    counter arm & chin with roll

286. Head pull from sit out position
    Over head grasp
    Set out grasp head with both hands—
        roll toward head
    Sit out to head drag flying mare
    Sit out & grab head
    Head wing
    Grab head & roll
    Pull head, both hands, turn to head side to
        break body hold
    Head pullover (pullback block)
    Grab head, twist & roll

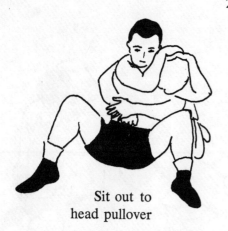

Sit out to
head pullover

287. Stand up
     Stand & wing
     Start of high wing
     Rump up
     Standing side roll
     Outside roll, standing
     Standing winglock
     Half-stand to roll, switch, sit out or
          complete stand-up
     Half standing roll
     High wing

Stand up

288. Crawfish
     Circling inward
     Back out
     Sit out & turn in
     Arm lift

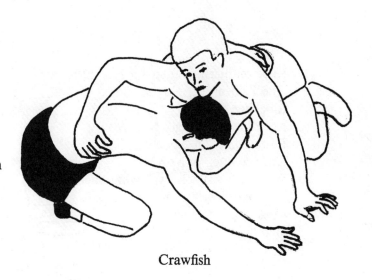

Crawfish

289. Over arm drag
     Arm check on turn in
     Meeting opponent
     Short arm drag to behind
     Reverse drag
     Dragging & moving toward sit out
     Over drag
     Arm hook & spin

Over drag to
counter crawfish

290. Double wristlock with grapevine
Double wristlock-leg keeps man parallel
Leg hook & double wristlock
Double wristlock with leg grapevine
Double wristlock
Double wristlock with outside leg grapevine
Side double wristlock with grapevine

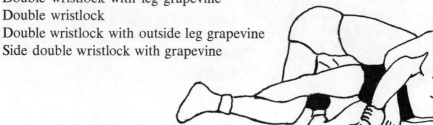

Double wristlock
with grapevine

291. Knee on bicep counter for No. 290
Kneel on arm
Blocking No. 290
Knee brace to break No. 290
Putting knee in No. 290
Knee counter to No. 290
Separate wristlock by driving knee
onto lower arm
Muscle grind block
Step on it

Knee break
counter to
double wristlock

292. Double wristlock with leg elevator
Double wristlock with leg lift
Double wristlock with elevator
Double wristlock with kickover
Double wristlock

Double wristlock
with elevator

116

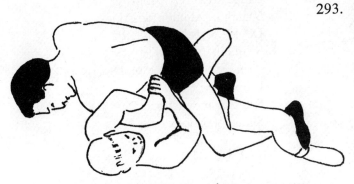

293. Double grapevine counter for No. 292
Double reverse grapevine
Stepping over No. 292 into straight
front scissor
Double leg stretch
Top body scissor
Double grapevine
Stretcher
Top body to double grapevine
Spread eagle var.

Double grapevine
counter for
double wristlock

294. Double wristlock elevator
Elevating arm & head pressure to reverse
Leg hook with double wrist lock
overhead scoot
Leg grapevine with laterally urift
Slipping a 1/2 nelson
Slip under wristlock
Over drag from No. 292
Under arm sneak
Under arm drag
Slip the half

Slipping under
arm with wristlock

295. Double wristlock with stepover
Double wristlock wing down for stepover
Step over wristlock
Wing & stepover

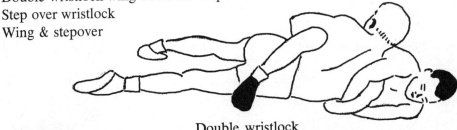

Double wristlock
& stepover

117

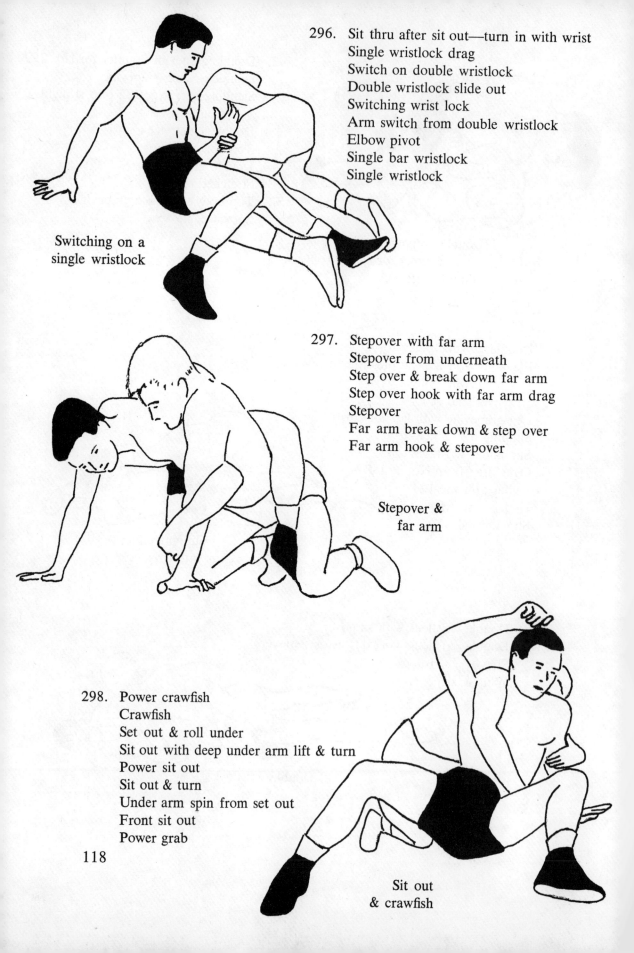

296. Sit thru after sit out—turn in with wrist
Single wristlock drag
Switch on double wristlock
Double wristlock slide out
Switching wrist lock
Arm switch from double wristlock
Elbow pivot
Single bar wristlock
Single wristlock

Switching on a
single wristlock

297. Stepover with far arm
Stepover from underneath
Step over & break down far arm
Step over hook with far arm drag
Stepover
Far arm break down & step over
Far arm hook & stepover

Stepover &
far arm

298. Power crawfish
Crawfish
Set out & roll under
Sit out with deep under arm lift & turn
Power sit out
Sit out & turn
Under arm spin from set out
Front sit out
Power grab

118

Sit out
& crawfish

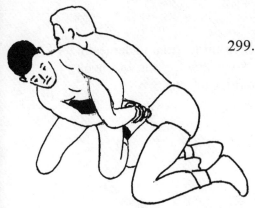

299. Inside double wristlock
     Double wristlock set through
     Lateral set out with double wristlock
     Near side double wristlock
     Double wristlock
     Double wristlock (knees & sitting)

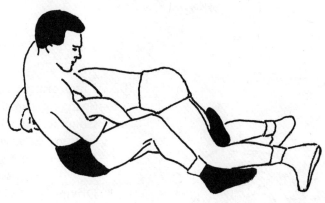

Inside double
wristlock with
leg hook

300. Side roll sit back
     Half stand and wing with knee block
     High wing
     Step out, sit up, hip roll
     High wing lock
     Outside roll var. half standing
     Winglock
     Step out, block near leg, side roll
     1/2 standing roll

Step out, wing
and turn in
hairpin turn-in

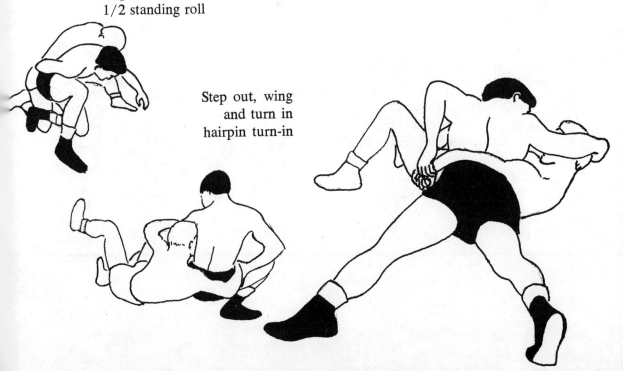

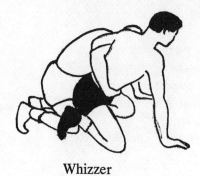

Whizzer

301. Whizzer hip throw from underneath
Whizzer (windmill or arm overhook)
Whizzer from ref. pos.
Windmill
Hiplock

Arm retreat
to counter
whizzer

302. Limp arm counter for whizzer
Swinging arm to remove whizzer
Counter hiplock by reaching back crotch
Slipping from whizzer
Whizzer counter with 1/2 nelson &
double bar
Driving into windmill
Counter to hiplock—pull out
Drop back arm to near leg
Ankle cross charge
Drag back

303. Arm pry counter for whizzer
Locking hands in prep. for head chancery
Counter for hiplock
Forward bar on whizzer
Locking hands and prying opponent's head down
Arm pry
Lock hands & bar arm forward (break leverage)
Shoulder pullunder

Arm pry counter
for whizzer

120

304. Head chancery & waist lock
1/2 nelson & bodylock
Double double counter for hiplock
Bear hug against whizzer
Bear hugging a windmill
Double double
1/2 nelson to counter whizzer

Double trouble
(or double)
counter for whizzer

305. Head up counter for No. 304
Bracing to prevent No. 304
Keep head up to prevent double double
Neck stretch against counter
Duck under & roll thru
Keeping head up
Head raise
Keep head high
D.D. Block

Head up
to prevent
double double

306. Head drag counter for No. 304
Sitting thru
Set thru
Sit thru with leg elevator
Duck under & roll thru
Turning into whizzer position
Head drag
Sit thru slip 1/2 nelson
Sit thru

Sit thru
to counter
double double

121

307. Roll under to counter whizzer

308. Whizzer with far arm
Whizzer & far arm
Hip-lock throw
Whizzer with cross arm drag
Whizzer
Windmill whizzor
Hip lock & far arm
Whizzer & far arm spike
Far arm whipover

Whizzer &
far arm

309. Pancake (counter for standing up
against whizzer)
Pancake
Whizzer spinner to lateral over & under
Whizzer (pancake), (under arm lock)
Whizzer
Hip lock spin to front throw
Whizzer move to front & use single bar
Whipover
Push—pull—twist

Pancake counter
for standing up
against whizzer

310. Roll thru with whizzer
Whizzer roll thru & leg lift
Over hook & elevator
Lateral roll under with elevator
Side roll from an over arm lock
Windmill whizzer with elevator
Hiplock & elevator
Reverse roll & elevator
Arm hook & elevator
Elevator (leg lift)

Whizzer &
elevator

311. Whizzer stiff arm
Reverse switch
Dropping the boom from overhook position
Whizzer with drift out
Reverse thigh
Windmill block
Hiplock & spin & over
Whizzer to inside crotch pry
Whizzer shrug block
Extended whizzer

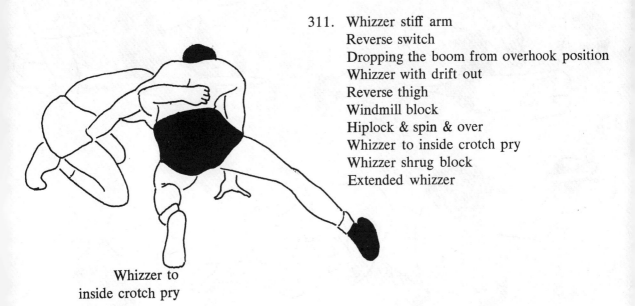

Whizzer to
inside crotch pry

312. Power switch
For sit out with downward arm drive
Sit out with under arm drag
Single arm drag from underneath
Set out & arm drag
Sit out
Power sit out

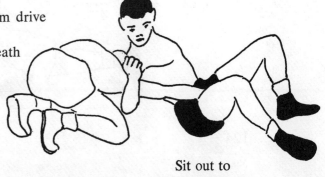

Sit out to
power switch

313. Sit out, turn in, with wrist to sit thru go behind
Sit out, turn out and back shoulder roll
Quarter set out with shoulder roll
Somersault escape
Sit out & forward roll
Sit out, forward roll, switch combination
Sit out & spin go behind
Sit out, turn under, backward roll,
    retain wrist to turn behind
Sit out—reverse somersault escape
Fake side roll—forward roll—return

Granby roll
sit out, roll in,
switch

314. Whizzer escape from over leg ride

315. Backwards cradle, wrist and leg roll

316. Over arm hook & slide out
Preventing TD by whizzering
Overhook, recover to hiplock
Whizzer check from under, with leg in
Over arm lock
Windmill
Hiplock by flattening opponent's legs
Caught on side, whizzer block with leg
"Graveyard" whizzer
Whizzer roll

Whizzer & slide out
to recover knees

317. Elevator with double leg grapevine
Leg hook-over head with hip scoot
Drifting laterally under arm
Double grapevine & arm lift
Slip under arm
Under arm drag
Slip under arm—with inside & outside
    leg grapevines
Under arm sneak
Elevator—throw arm

Slip under arm
with inside &
outside grapevines

318. Arm drag with elevator
Sliding arm & tailing
Elevator with arm drag
Arm drag with elevator
Arm drag & elevate
Arm drag from underneath
Double arm drag & elevator
Arm drag & elevator
Sitting double arm drag
Elevator—bend arm

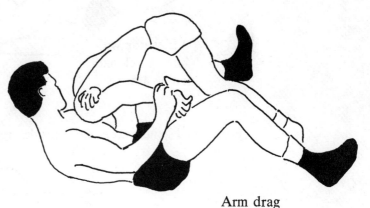

Arm drag
with elevator

319. Arm drag counter for single leg pickup
Lateral back creeper
Arm drag & pull around
Scooting out
Double arm drag & scoot behind
Arm drag using leg hook to help
    force opp. past
Arm drag & leg bar
Drag

← Back of knee

Arm drag and
pull around

320. Reverse elevator
Leg lift & knee block with whipover
Elevator
Leg elevators with scissor action laterally
Elevator with double arm lock
Elevator flip
Corkscrew elevator
Elevator roll

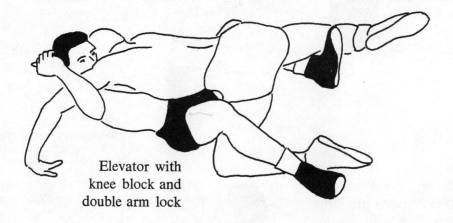

Elevator with
knee block and
double arm lock

321. Force head behind to counter inside crotch ride

322. Close tieup (standing neutral)
Closed stance—neck and elbow
Head to head tieup
Neck and elbow tieup
Closed stance
Locked horns—or referee's position

Closed stance—neck & elbow

323. Open stance—ready
Square stance
Square stance—Faceoff

Open stance

324. Under arm tieup
Upper arm tie (black)
Semi-open stance
Inside grip on arms
Square stance—double elbow grasp

129

Double biceps

325. Over-hook tieup
     Closed stance—head out
     Neck—over arm tie
     Referee's position—Arm grapevine grasp

Neck and over arm

326. Double wrist tieup
     Inside and outside grip
     Inside wrist control
     Semi-open stance—wrist deep
     Inside wrist grip
     Square stance—double wrist grasp

Inside and outside wrist

327. Muscle tieup
     Neck and muscle tieup
     Closed stance—collar and inside elbow
     Neck and inside grip
     Referee's position—bicep grasp

Neck and muscle

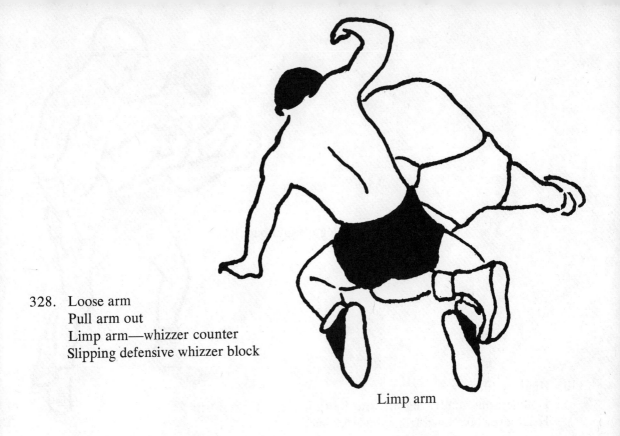

328. Loose arm
     Pull arm out
     Limp arm—whizzer counter
     Slipping defensive whizzer block

Limp arm

329. Head snap (sideways)
     Head snap to single leg dive
     Snap down
     Head pop
     Right arm "shrug" from referee's position

131

Head snap

Single leg lift and back heel

330.  High leg lift
       Double arm—under leg lift with foot kick (1) Pickup trip
       Head lever takedown from single leg pickup
       Single leg lift—both hands outside
       "Tree-topping" a leg (1)
       Leg lift standing to back heel (1)

Knee lock takedown (3)

331.  Knee pressure takedown (No. 3)
       Knee lock (3)
       Lock knee and fall back
       Single leg to rear dump
       Bear weight against knee to drop to mat, ready for cradle

Duck under

332. Head drag
Duck under
Head drag from duck under
Duck under
Duck under

Fore and aft—counter for
foot in crotch

333. Split leg pressure takedown (1)
Between legs knee lock
High single leg trap (takedown)
Hold opponent's leg in crotch with both hands
Foot dump—(leg in crotch)
Counter for leg in crotch, counter for single leg (fore and aft)

334. Split leg pressure takedown (2)
Between legs knee lock (2)
High single leg trap (takedown) (2)
Set back to weak side from 333
Foot dump-leg in crotch (2)
Drop to knees for "fore and aft" takedown

133

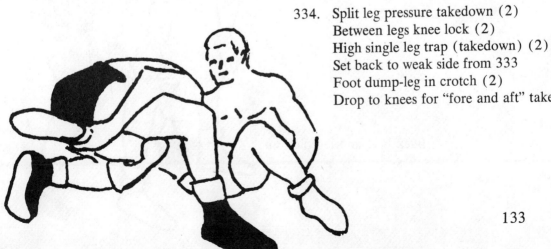

Fore and aft takedown

335. Reverse quarter nelson and hip lock
Body press (from front quarter nelson and far arm)
Whizzer pin
Double over—arm bar (pin)
Cross arm and body press—pin

Body press from front
quarter nelson and
far arm

336. Crotch lift (behind standing)
Back heel and leg pick up
Rear thigh lift
Rear waist and crotch dump
Under knee hook for back takedown

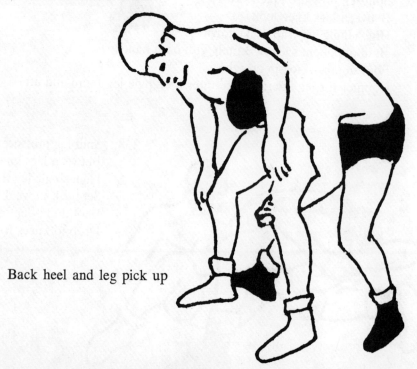

Back heel and leg pick up

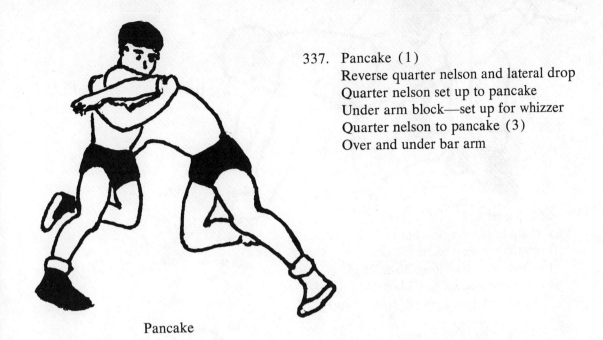

337. Pancake (1)
    Reverse quarter nelson and lateral drop
    Quarter nelson set up to pancake
    Under arm block—set up for whizzer
    Quarter nelson to pancake (3)
    Over and under bar arm

Pancake

338. Leg in thigh lift
    Far ankle to over and under
    Far ankle pickup to crotch ride
    Far leg pick up
    Crotch breakdown to Oklahoma ride
    Far ankle pick up to cross crotch reverse pin

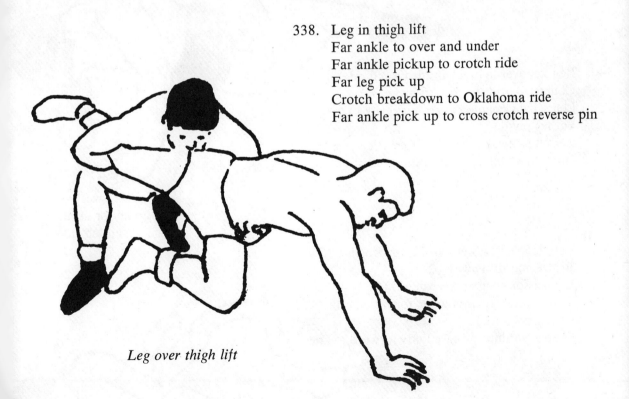

*Leg over thigh lift*

135

Bottom ankle pick up

339. Split leg pry (1)
    Far ankle to over and under
    Far ankle pickup to crotch ride
    Pull bottom ankle from 36 to inside crotch
    Crotch breakdown to Oklahoma ride
    Far ankle pickup to cross crotch reverse pin

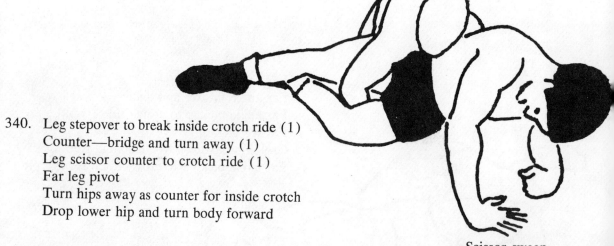

340. Leg stepover to break inside crotch ride (1)
    Counter—bridge and turn away (1)
    Leg scissor counter to crotch ride (1)
    Far leg pivot
    Turn hips away as counter for inside crotch
    Drop lower hip and turn body forward

Scissor sweep—
break for inside
crotch ride

341. Leg stepover to break inside crotch ride (2)
    Bridge and turn away (2)
    Leg scissor counter to crotch ride (2)
    Turn hips away as counter for inside crotch (2)
    Far leg pivot (2)
    Drop lower hip and turn body forward to knees

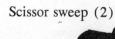

Scissor sweep (2)

136

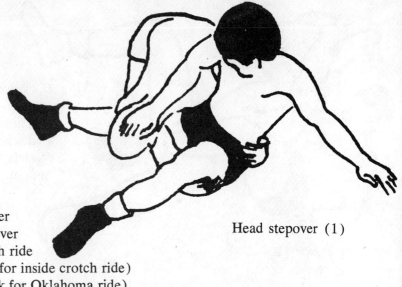

342. Head push and leg stepover
Push head and throw leg over
Step over counter to crotch ride
Push head down (counter for inside crotch ride)
Leg over head pivot (break for Oklahoma ride)
Slip hips out

Head stepover (1)

343. Head push and leg stepover (2)
Push head and throw leg over (2)
Step over counter to crotch ride (2)
Step over when head is down—continuation of 342
Leg over head (2)
Step over head with free leg—turning into opponent

Head stepover (2)

Stretcher escape (1)—roll to left and take foot

344. Back door escape from double leg ride
Pull leg overhead (1)
Left lift and turn in
Pull up leg to start escape
Stretcher break
Sitting position (slipping out of over scissors)

137

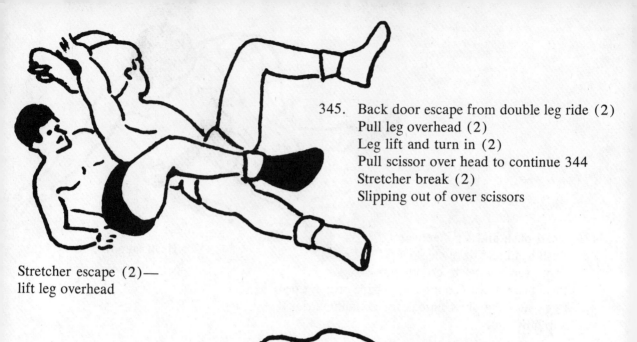

345. Back door escape from double leg ride (2)
Pull leg overhead (2)
Leg lift and turn in (2)
Pull scissor over head to continue 344
Stretcher break (2)
Slipping out of over scissors

Stretcher escape (2)—
lift leg overhead

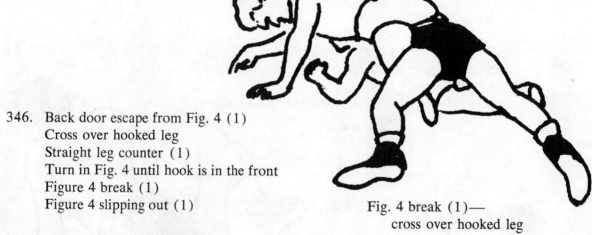

346. Back door escape from Fig. 4 (1)
Cross over hooked leg
Straight leg counter (1)
Turn in Fig. 4 until hook is in the front
Figure 4 break (1)
Figure 4 slipping out (1)

Fig. 4 break (1)—
cross over hooked leg

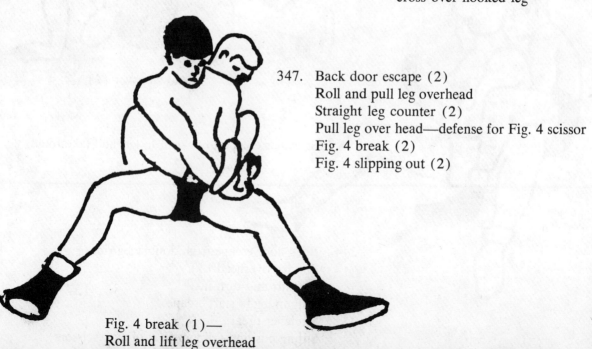

347. Back door escape (2)
Roll and pull leg overhead
Straight leg counter (2)
Pull leg over head—defense for Fig. 4 scissor
Fig. 4 break (2)
Fig. 4 slipping out (2)

Fig. 4 break (1)—
Roll and lift leg overhead

348. Cross ride, far arm under hook
Turn in and bridge out (counter to cross body)
Cross body and near leg grapevine ride
Cross body ride with under arm hook
Straight arm break (from knees for guillotine)
Slipping out of cross body (1)

Cross body ride—under arm hook

Straight arm cross body break—turn in and bridge out

349. Breaking Cross ride
Turn in and bridge out (2)
Inside arm—clear counter to grapevine
Drill to loosen cross body ride
Straight arm break (2)
Slipping out of cross body (2)

139

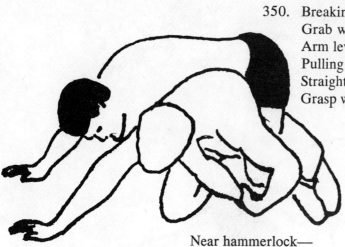

350. Breaking cross ride with back arm pressure (1)
Grab wrist and turn in (counter to cross body)
Arm lever counter to grapevine (1)
Pulling arm loose on opponent's cross body ride
Straight arm break (guillotine on mat) (1)
Grasp wrist, sit through to reverse arm lock

Near hammerlock—
break for cross body or leg split (1)

Near hammerlock (2)

351. Breaking cross ride with back arm pressure (2)
Grab wrist and turn in (2)
Arm lever counter to grapevine (2)
Drill when turning in from 350
Straight arm break (2)
Slip behind

352. Head lock—counter to cross body
Head lock as defense for cross body
Head-pull break (guillotine) (1)
Cross body ride—headlock pull through

140

Head lock—counter to guillotine (1)

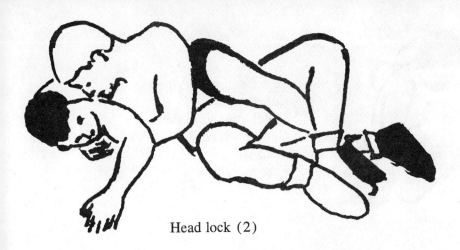

Head lock (2)

353. Head lock—counter to cross body
Head lock as defense for cross body turning on top
Head pull break (2)
Head lock pull through (2)

354. "Tailing out" from Jacob arm hook and grapevine (1)
Arm drag—counter for cross body and reverse arm hook
Arm drag (Turk break)
Arm drag out of Turk ride
Arm grapevine ride—sit through and cross arm drag

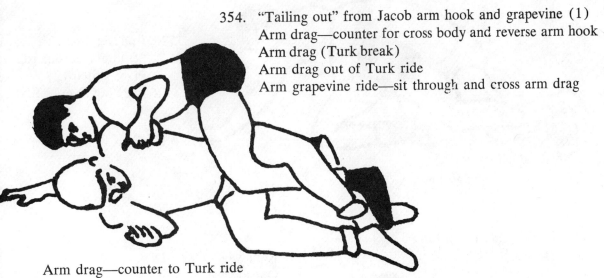

Arm drag—counter to Turk ride

355. Tailing out from Jacob arm hook and grapevine (2)
Arm drag counter for cross body and reverse arm hook
Arm drag counter to "Turk" (2)
Arm drag—Turk break (2)
Arm drag out of Turk ride (2)
Slip behind

Arm drag as counter (2)

356. Switch with grapevine
Inside switch
Switch counter to stepover
Outside switch with leg hooked from inside
Pivot switch (1)
Fake switch move

Inside switch with grapevine

357. Runaway switch (1)
Set up for outside roll
Pivot switch (2)
Back out or crawfish

Running switch

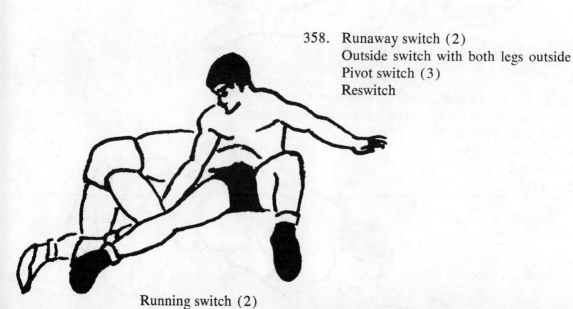

358. Runaway switch (2)
Outside switch with both legs outside
Pivot switch (3)
Reswitch

Running switch (2)

Granby roll (1)*

359. Sitting come back wing with opposite side leg
Forward or Granby roll (1)
Arm and far leg roll (1)
Hip roll to reverse cradle (1)

360. Sitting come back with opposite side leg (2)
Forward or Granby roll from short sit out
Grasping leg on Granby roll
Arm and far leg roll (2)
Hip roll to reverse cradle (2)

Granby roll (2)

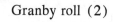

Sit out and turn out (1)

361. Sit out and hip heist
Outside arm (roll)
Sit out to reverse face off (1)

* See bottom page 13.

143

362.  Sit out and hip heist (2)
      Outside arm (2)
      Sit out to reverse face off (2)

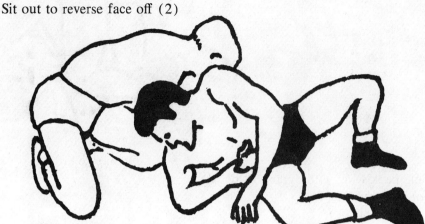

Sit out and turn out (2)

363.  Overhook (1), whizzer back over (wing) to cradle
      Hip lock and cradle
      Counter to roll—through counter of whizzer (1)
      Driving opponent down with whizzer
      "Roll through" (1)
      Crawfish cradle from underneath (1)

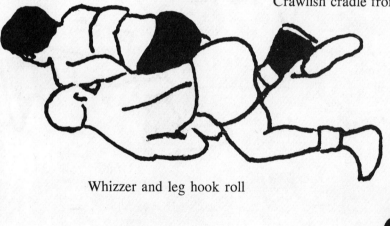

Whizzer and leg hook roll

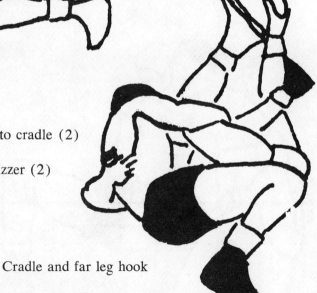

364.  Overhook whizzer, back over (wing) to cradle (2)
      Hip lock and cradle (2)
      Counter to roll through counter of whizzer (2)
      Cradle pin from whizzer series
      "Roll through" (2)
      Crawfish cradle from underneath (2)

Cradle and far leg hook

144

365. Stand up arm removal (1)
Tripod stand up and turn away (near leg) (1)
Inside leg stand up
Slipping the hand off to face off

Stand up with inside leg (1)

366. Stand up arm removal (2)
Tripod stand up and turn away (near leg) (2)
Controlling hands on inside leg stand up (2)
Slipping the hand off to face off (2)

Stand up with inside leg (2)

367. Stand up arm spread (1)
Tripod stand up, turn in (far leg) (1)
Outside leg stand up
Two-on-one stand up escape (1)
Peeling out (1)

Stand up with outside leg (1)

145

368.  Stand up arm spread (2)
Tripod stand up, turn in (far leg) (2)
Controlling hands on stand up
Two-on-one stand up (2)
Peeling out (2)

Stand up with outside leg (2)

369.  Split leg switch (1)
Counter for crossover on switch—leg block (1)
Standard switch (1)
Outside switch
"Leg spread" switch

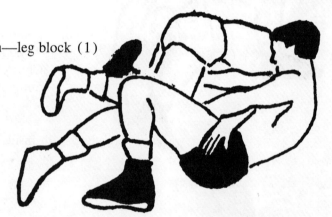

Stepover counter on switch (1)—block far leg

Stepover counter (2) turn on top

370.  Split leg switch (2)
Counter for cross over on switch—leg block (2)
Standard switch (2)
Flattening opponent and turning on top from outside switch
"Leg spread switch" (2)

146

Stepover counter (1)—behind thigh grip

371. Body throwover (1)
Counter for crossover—bridge over (1)
Leg elevator to step across switch counter (1)
Start of back roll (when opponent steps over switch)
Elevator (stepover block)
Switch—step over—loop back

372. Body throw over (2)
Counter for cross over (2)
Leg elevator to step across switch counter (2)
Inside crotch as finish for 371
Elevator (2)
Switch—step over loop back (2)

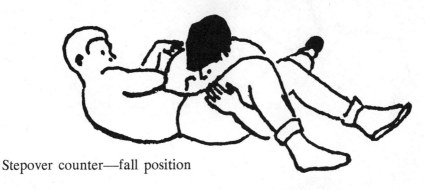

Stepover counter—fall position

373. Switch counter—loose arm
Pull arm out
Crotch ride
Jerk arm out of outside switch
Checking switch—crotch stepover slip behind

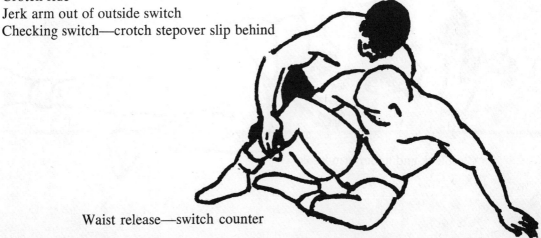

Waist release—switch counter

374. Switch, over leg hook, tail around
Counter for leg switch
Drive opponent's head in mat
Leg spread switch
Checking switch crotch, stepover, slip behind leg lift

Counter leg switch—forward roll

375. Switch leg hook, tail around and rear crotch drive (2)
Counter for leg switch (2)
Finish on top from 374
Leg spread switch (2)
Checking switch crotch, step over behind (2)

Counter leg switch forward roll, slip behind

376. Underarm check and chin hold on sit out and tur
Head lock and arm hook
Jerk back with chin and arm tieup from sit out
Reverse arm hook and chin lock

Chin lock and under arm hook

148

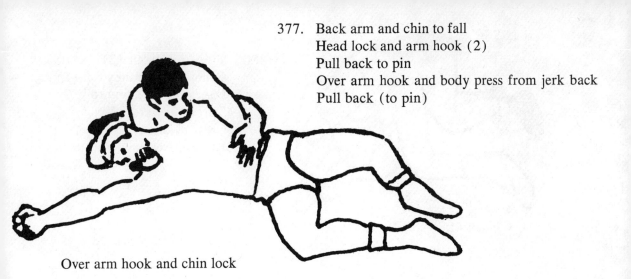

377. Back arm and chin to fall
Head lock and arm hook (2)
Pull back to pin
Over arm hook and body press from jerk back
Pull back (to pin)

Over arm hook and chin lock

378. Under arm check, circle head to bar arm and chancery
Snap back and double double
Underhook and change bar (1)
Jerk back with chin and arm tieup from sit out
Pull back (2)
Reverse arm hook and chin

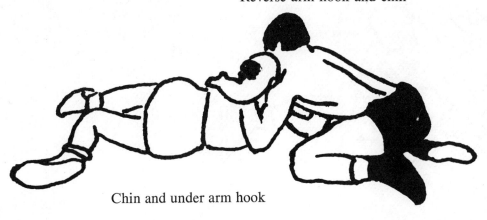

Chin and under arm hook

379. Under arm check, circle head to bar arm and chancery (2)
Snap back (2) and double double (2)
Underhook (2) and change bar to elbow hook to bar (2)
Pin with half nelson and body lock from 378
Bar arm and half nelson

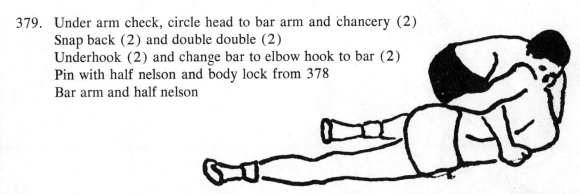

Pin with half nelson and body lock from 378

380. Sit and back out (2)
    Counter for Granby roll (1)
    Forward or Granby roll (2)
    Start of forward roll
    Cross pivot (1)
    Hip roll from underneath (1)

Follow roll (1)—counter to Granby

381. Counter for Granby roll (2)
    Forward for Granby roll (2)
    Forward roll
    Cross pivot (2)
    Counter hip roll (1)

Follow roll (2)—counter to Granby

382. Far arm and headlock
    Counter for hip lock—arm lock and double double
    Deep half counter to whizzer
    3/4 nelson
    Near arm and half nelson
    Bar arm and half nelson

Double double or
bar arm and half nelson—
counter to whizzer

383. Leg counter on arm roll (outside leg)
Counter to winglock—back of knee pickup
Blocking outside roll by hooking top knee
Leg lift block
Sit through counter to 382

Leg lift—counter to winglock

384. Leg counter on arm roll—inside legs
Counter to winglock—cross over
Block outside roll with inside crotch ride
Counter for cross crotch

Inside crotch—counter to winglock

385. Standup counter—back knee pick up
Block stand up with waist and thigh lift
Half up, knee and foot position (counter to 384)

151

Thigh lift—counter to stand up

Chicken wing and under arm hook

386. Bar arm to head scissors
Chicken wing and Fig. 4 head scissors
Over and under double bar
Turning opponent with chicken wing and under arm hook
Near bar arm

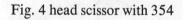

387. Bar arm to head scissors (2)
Chicken wing and Fig. 4 head scissors (2)
With Fig. 4 head scissors (2)
Over and under with Fig. 4 head scissor 354
Fig. 4 head scissors

Fig. 4 head scissor with 354

388. Double bar arm (1)
Double arm bar and walk around (1)
Double reverse bar arm up the back
Double over-hook pin (1)
Double back bar arm around the head pin (1)

152            Double arm bar

Double arm bar and sit through

389.  Double bar arm (2)
Double arm bar and walk around (2)
Double reverse arm bar up the back to pin (2)
Double over-hook pin (2)
Double back bar arm around the head pin (2)

390.  Finish fall from Fig. 4 scissors and head
Figure 4 pin
Figure 4 scissor with head hold
Figure 4 under half nelson trap

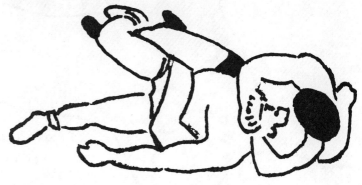

Fig. 4 Guillotine

391.  Reverse stretcher and reverse hiplock
Double grapevine with near arm tieup
Double leg grapevine and arm
Double ankle hook and arm grapevine

Double grapevine with near arm hook

153

392. Back arm bar to fall
    Over arm hook to reverse nelson
    Reverse bar on top arm
    Arm hook and reverse nelson (1)
    Far arm reverse hook
    Michigan fulcrum

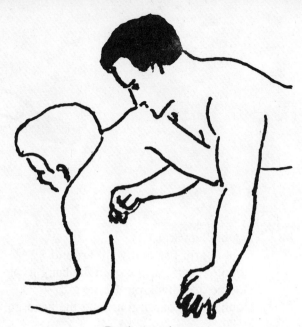

Back arm bar

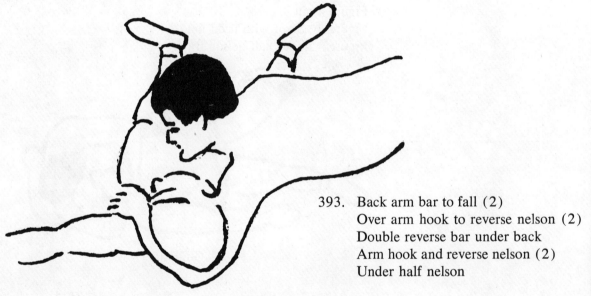

Back arm bar and reverse nelson

393. Back arm bar to fall (2)
    Over arm hook to reverse nelson (2)
    Double reverse bar under back
    Arm hook and reverse nelson (2)
    Under half nelson

394. Head duck under on mat to half nelson (1)
    Head and arm lever to duck under (1)
    Head lever and waist lock
    Double double (1)
    Neck bar arm
    Arm lift to walk around (1)

154

Arm lift to half nelson

395. Head duck under on mat to half nelson (2)
Head and arm lever to duck under (2)
Half nelson and waist lock
Double double (2)
Deep half nelson
Arm lift to walk around (2)

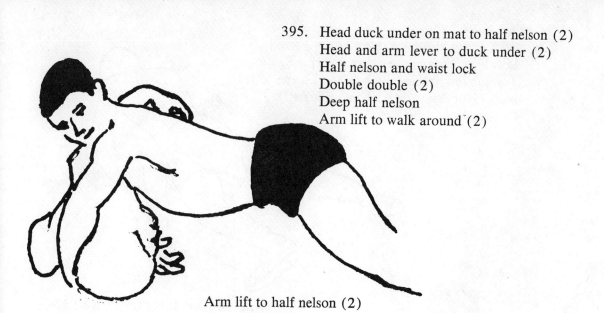

Arm lift to half nelson (2)

396. Cross body foot release
Slipping a leg—toeing it loose

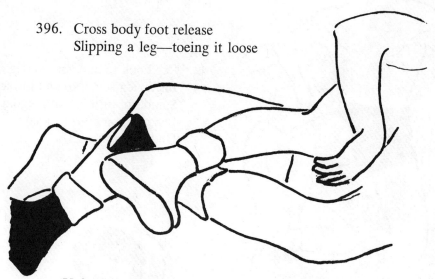

Unhooking grapevine cross body ride escape

397. Back out of inside leg ride (1)
Low leg scissor counter to crotch ride (1)
Turning into inside crotch ride as escape (1)
Back pivot escape (Oklahoma ride) (1)
Deep crotch and waist

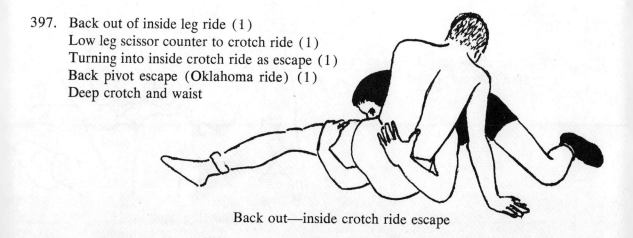

Back out—inside crotch ride escape

398. Back out of inside leg ride (2)
    Low leg scissor counter to crotch ride (2)
    Turning into inside crotch ride as escape (2)
    Back pivot escape (Oklahoma ride) (2)
    Drifting from drop

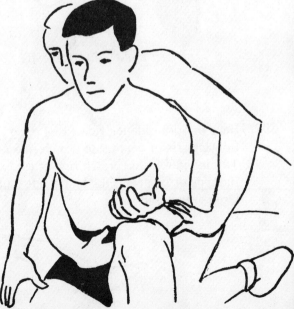

Back out—inside crotch escape (2)

399. Leg hook to counter overleg ride
    Inside leg stand up and inward pivot
    Stand up, turn in, with leg hooked
    Inside leg and arm standing
    Under arm hook

Leg lever—counter to overleg ride

400. Close elbow preparatory to stand up
    Start of cross peel off

156

Inside leg stand up (1)

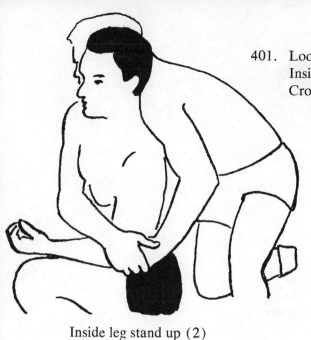

401. Loosening opponent's control grip
Inside leg stand up—preventing locked hands
Cross peel off

Inside leg stand up (2)

402. Hand control with stand up
Inside leg stand up—two on one (hands)
Double hand push

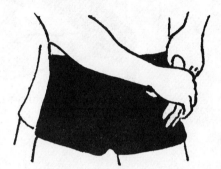

Inside leg stand up (3)

403. Force hand behind and secure other with stand up
Inside leg stand up—pulling one hand loose
Over grasp of hand

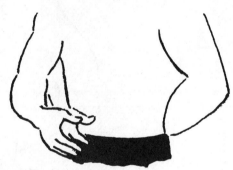

Inside leg stand up (4)

404. Remove both hands to go free
Completion of 403
Double peel off

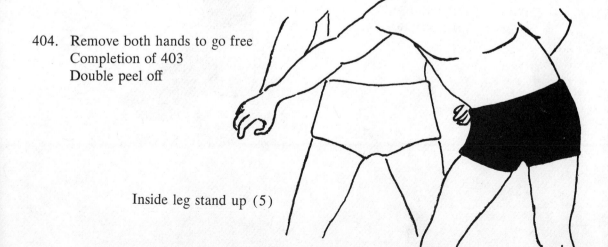

Inside leg stand up (5)

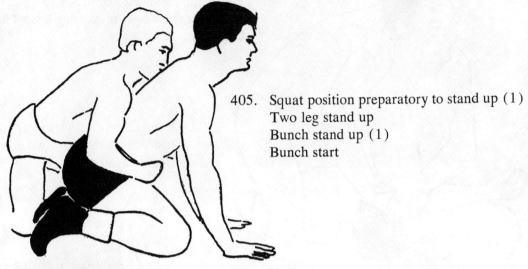

405. Squat position preparatory to stand up (1)
Two leg stand up
Bunch stand up (1)
Bunch start

Bump back stand up (1)

406. Squat position preparatory to stand up (2)
Two leg stand up (2)
"Bunch" stand up (2)
Blow to squat position

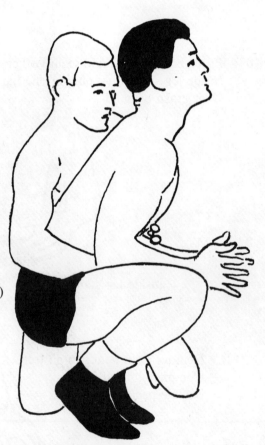

Bump back stand up (2)

158

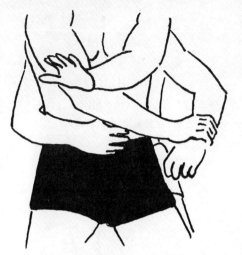

407. Breaking hands loose
"Bunch" stand up (3)
Cross wrist push off

Bump back stand up (3)

408. Breaking hands loose
"Bunch" stand up (4)

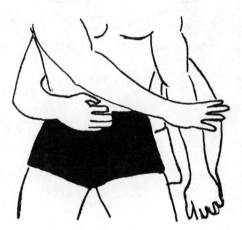

Bump back stand up (4)

409. "Bunch" stand up (5)
Over grasp

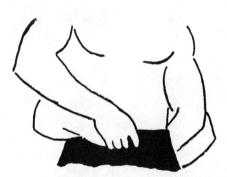

Bump back stand up (5)

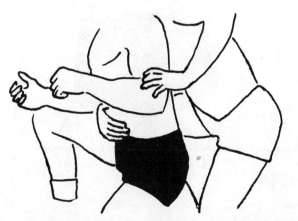

410. Position of hands
Over grasp (1)

Outside leg stand up (1)

159

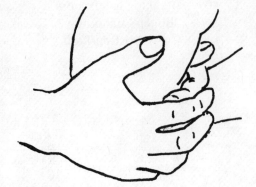

Outside leg stand up (2)—wrestlers' hands

411. Removing elbow grip
Wrestlers' hands
Over grasp

412. Hand behind
Two-on-one (hands)
Over grasp

Outside leg stand up (3)

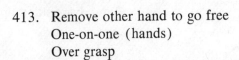

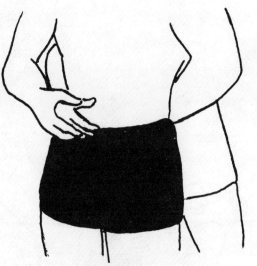

413. Remove other hand to go free
One-on-one (hands)
Over grasp

Outside leg stand up (4)

414. Standing wing or arm roll (grasping wrist)
Cross arm side roll (1)
Half stand outside roll
Half stand cross arm roll (1)
Sprinter's start sit through

Standing wing (grasping hand)

415. Cross arm side roll (2)
Half stand out side roll (2)
Half stand cross arm roll (2)
Sprinter's start sit through

Standing wing

416. Back breaker (1)
Hands position on stand up
Step behind dump (1)
Reverse double leg pick up (1)

161

Step behind and double leg pick up (arm lift to free body)

Step behind and double leg pick up (2)

417. Back breaker (2)
Step behind and double leg pick up from 416
Step behind dump (2)
Reverse double leg pick up

418. Cross face
Cross face cradle (1)
Cross face far ankle ride
Side cradle (1)
Cross arm attack to cradle

Far cradle from cross face (1)

419. Cross face cradle (2)
Cross face to far leg cradle (2)
Cross cradle from 418
Side cradle (2)
Cross arm attack to cradle (2)

162

Far cradle and leg (2)

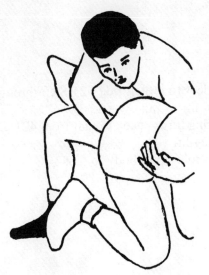

420. Near leg pick up to crotch lift
Near leg pick up
Near leg lift
Near leg pick up to reverse cross crotch

Near leg lift to thigh

421. Near leg lift to thigh (2)
Near leg pick up to crotch lift (2)
Near leg lift (2)
Near leg pick up to reverse cross crotch (2)

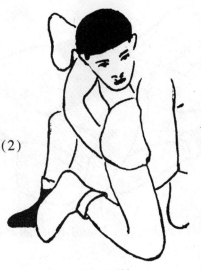

Crotch lift

422. Twist legs to crotch ride
Near leg pick up to crotch lift (3)
Near leg lift (3)
Stand up to execute reverse cross crotch

Turning opponent from crotch lift

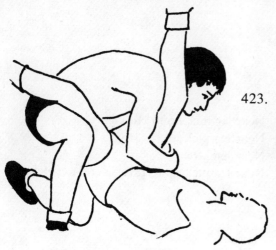

423. Twist legs to crotch ride (2) Step through
Crotch lift to fall
Checking turn—back to mat from 421 and 422
Near leg lift (4)
Crotch fold-up to body to 424

Push down—back to mat

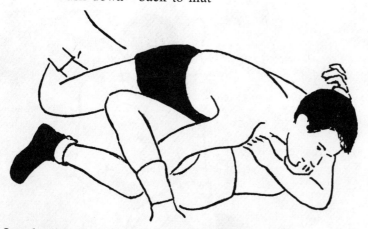

Leg hook, reverse crotch and half nelson—fall from near leg lift and step through

424. Fall from near leg lift and step through
Pin from crotch lift series 420 to 423
Near leg lift (5)
Crotch fold up of body

425. Reverse crotch pick-up to 426

Far leg lift

426.  Turning far leg lift

Far leg lift (2)

427.  Far leg lift (3) to fall
      Lower body lift
      Pin effort from far leg lift
      Crotch pick up—lift buttocks off mat

For leg lift to push down

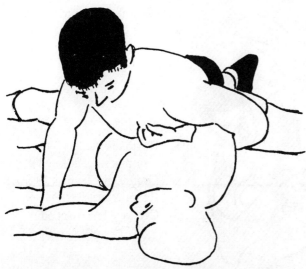

428.  Underarm check and bar
      Bottom arm
      Single over-arm bar
      Arm grapevine and body press

165

Arm lock and body press

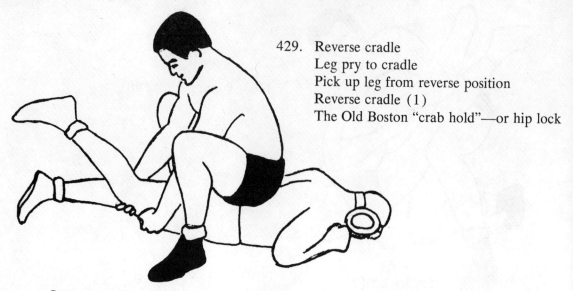

429. Reverse cradle
Leg pry to cradle
Pick up leg from reverse position
Reverse cradle (1)
The Old Boston "crab hold"—or hip lock

Leg turnover to cradle (1)—also crab hold

430. Reverse cradle (2)
Leg pry to cradle (2)
Lock knee and turn from 429
Reverse cradle (2)
Lateral leg pick up from 429 to cradle (leg trapped)

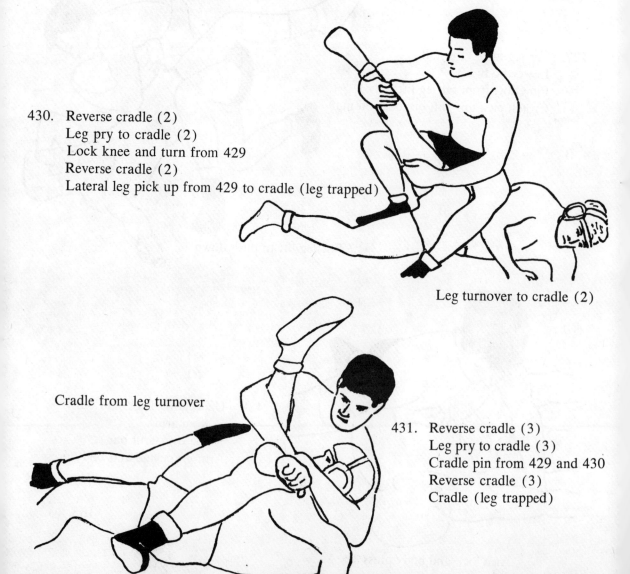

Leg turnover to cradle (2)

Cradle from leg turnover

431. Reverse cradle (3)
Leg pry to cradle (3)
Cradle pin from 429 and 430
Reverse cradle (3)
Cradle (leg trapped)

432. Guillotine block and counter (1)

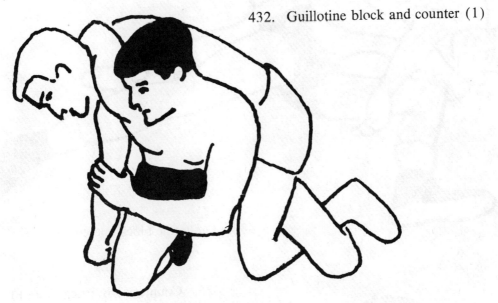

Block arm and rotate leg

433. Guillotine block and counter (2)

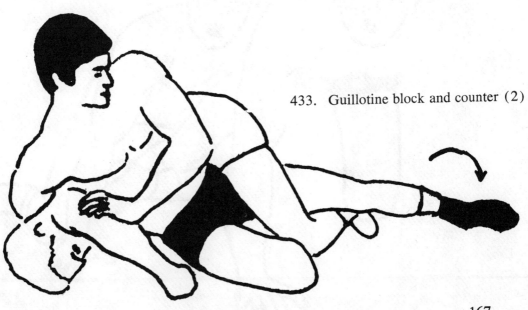

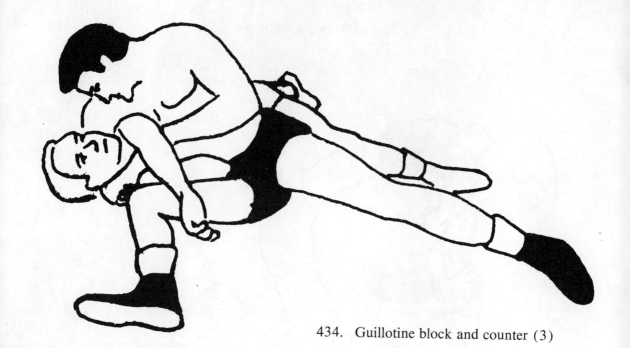

434.  Guillotine block and counter (3)

435.  Countering over leg side (1)

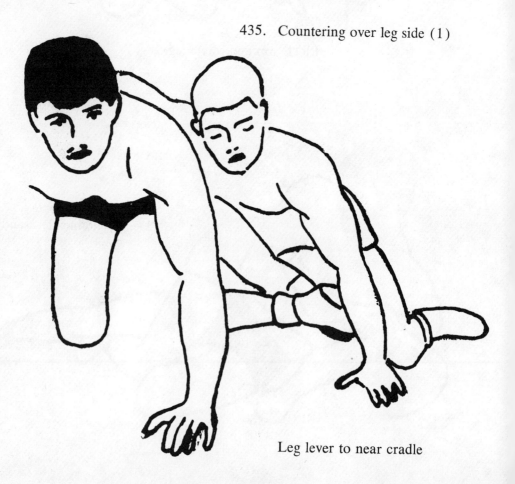

Leg lever to near cradle

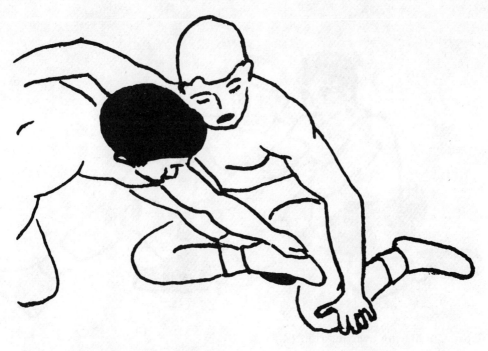

436.   Countering over leg ride (2)

437.   Countering over leg ride (3)

169

438. Countering over leg ride (4)

439. Countering over leg ride (5)

170

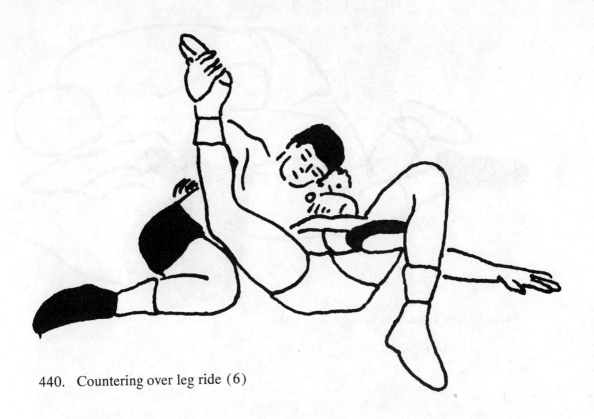

440.  Countering over leg ride (6)

441.  Escape from arm through legs (1)

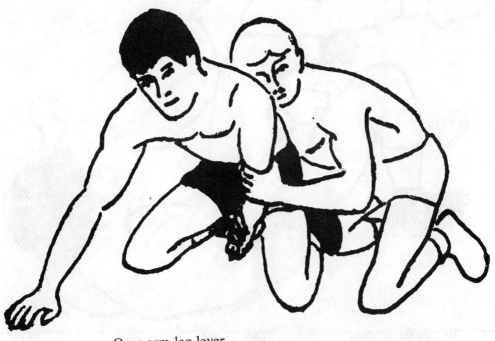

Over arm leg lever

442. Escape from arm through legs (2)

443. Escape from arm through legs (3)

172

444. Escape from arm through legs (4)

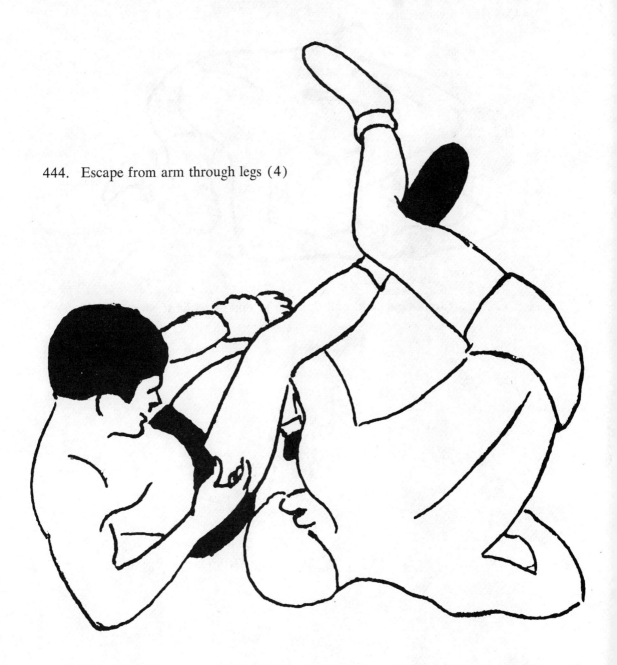

445. Head lever escape

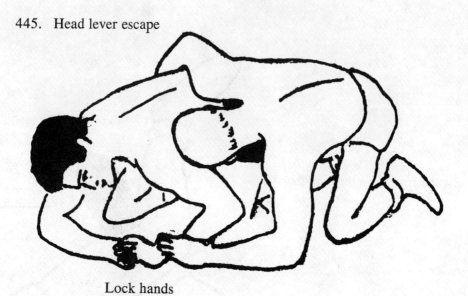

Lock hands

(Join hands and pull through to opposite side to switch position)

# Sources of Illustrations

Bureau of Aeronautics (U.S.), Navy Dept., *Wrestling*, Annapolis, 1943, U.S. Naval Inst.

Cann, Wilfred Edward, *Manual of Wrestling*, Battle Creek, Mich., Hygiene and Physical Education Press, 1912.

*Championship Wrestling*, Keen, Speidel and Swartz, U.S. Naval Inst., Annapolis, 1961.

Gallagher, Edward C., *Wrestling*, 1925, 1927.

Gallagher, E. C., and Peery, Rex, 1939, A.S. Barnes and Co., 1951, N.Y., The Ronald Press Co.

Kenney, Harold E., and Law, Glenn C. ("Newt"), McGraw-Hill, N.Y., 1952.

Leonard, Hugh F., *A Handbook of Wrestling*, E. R. Pelton, N.Y., 1897.

Martin, Bill, pictures selected from movies.

Otopalik, Hugo, *Modern Wrestling for High School and College*, N.Y., Chas. Scribner's Sons, 1930.

Schall, Jim—separate pictures.

Sparks, Raymond, *A Syllabus of Wrestling*.

Stone, Henry A., *Wrestling, Intercollegiate and Olympic*.

Umbach, Arnold W., and Johnson, Warren, *Successful Wrestling*, 1953, C. V. Mosby, St. Louis.

V-Five Association, Annapolis, Md. 1950, *Wrestling*, U.S. Naval Institute.

Vorres, Spyros K., *Wrestle to Win*, Chicago, 1930.

Zapasy Klasyczne Iwolne, Warszawa, 1956, Sport I Turystyka. N. M. Galkowski, A. Z. Katulin, N. G. Czionow.

Regretfully, the following books had been taken from the shelves in the Library of Congress and not returned:

Bishop, William Austin, *Free-Style Wrestling*, N.Y., 1939, American Sports Pub. Co.

Bothner, George, *Scientific Wrestling,* Richard K. Fox Pub. Co., 1912. (Among professional wrestlers of an almost forgotten era, Bothner was rated as the most scientific wrestler of all time.)

McMahon, Donald Vincent, *Fundamentals of High School Wrestling,* Golden, Colo., 1951.

Of the more than 100 books examined at the Library of Congress about 60 are listed on other pages. Many of these books have value for the student of Free Style and Greco-Roman Wrestling. However, as an encyclopedia of American-style wrestling compiled for the express purpose of giving a common language to the high school and college wrestling coaches of this country it seemed advisable not to attempt to include these Olympic styles. It may be that in a revised edition a special section may be added.

# Bibliography

(*Most books in Library of Congress*)

*A.A.U. Wrestling Guides*

Alikhanov, I., *Borba Volnaia,* 1956 (Russian). This book shows the American influence. It is well illustrated and shows much American style wrestling, particularly takedowns.

Armstrong, Sir, Walter, London, 1897.

Begala, Joe, Film No. 1: *Takedowns from Standing Position* and Film No. 2: *Counters for Takedowns from Standing Position.* (EDcom Productions, 26991 Tungsten Rd., Cleveland, Ohio).

Bishop, William Austin, *Free-Style Wrestling.* Illustrations by Ben and Richard Bishop. N.Y., American Sports Publishing Company, 1939. This book is missing.

Borisov, Isaak Borisovich, *Na Bortsovskom kovre,* 1956.

Bothner, George, *Scientific Wrestling,* 161 p. Richard K. Fox Pub. Co., 1912. It is a great loss that this book is not on the shelves of the Library and has not been for 30 years. George Bothner is considered by old-time professionals to be the most scientific wrestler who ever lived. For years, he maintained a gym on 42nd Street not far from Broadway in New York, where all professionals who were really good wrestlers used to go to work out with each other.

Bulgaria, *Sustezaleini pravila po gruko-rimska borba,* 76 p.

Cann, Wilfred Edward, *Manual of Wrestling,* Battle Creek, Mich., Hygiene and Physical Education Press, 1912, 217 p. This is the best book of its era and certainly better than anything that came before. It is sound, fundamental wrestling. Changes in rules have since made some maneuvers too risky to use.

Carson, Ray F. and Buel R. Patterson, *Principles of Championship Wrestling* (South Brunswick, New Jersey: A. S. Barnes and Co., 1972).

Colombia, *Reglamentos oficiales de boxeo, lucha libre, levantamiento de pesos.* Arreglo del Prof. Alberto Gomez Moreno, Bogota Imprenta Nacional, 1944. This is merely a Colombian wrestling and boxing guide with rules.

Curley, Jack, *Modern Wrestling.* 150 illustrations, New York City. The Ring Book Shop. A book about professional wrestlers and wrestling. College and high school coaches will find little of value here since most of the holds shown are barred in amateur wrestling.

Cygeniewicz, Stanislaw Zybszko, *Na ringach calego swiata hsiezo wspomnien Warszawa,* Zalkl, 1937. Stanislaw Zbysko and his brother Vladek are well known and respected throughout the wrestling world (professional). Both are college men. No illustrations.

Delbridge, James, *Delbridge's Guide on Grab Hold or Cornish Style of Wrestling,* Neshannock, Pa. 1879. Hilarious.

Dick (William Brisbane) *Dick's Art of Wrestling,* N.Y., Dick and Fitzgerald 1887. Standing holds, throws only.

Dörr, Wilhelm, *Ringkampf in Bildern und Merkworten,* Stuttgart, Dieck & Co. 1924. Good illustrations on Free-Style wrestling but no material for coaches. German.

Fleischer, Nathaniel S., *From Milo to Londos,* The story of wrestling through the ages. Illustrated N.Y. City Press of C. J. O'Brien. Inc., 1936. All about professionals—no holds shown.

Gallagher, Edward Clark. Ed Gallagher's three books on wrestling are well-known. His first was illustrated with small, inferior photographs but they brought something new to the world of wrestling books. Pictures were of actual wrestling and not posed. New material was presented on counter wrestling. From certain statements made by the author, it can be seen that this book contained but a small part of his teachings. It is doubtful whether this work was ever edited. Probably this was a fortunate oversight, for the homely philosophy and western humor of Ed Gallagher might have been edited out. All Gallagher's books are good.

Geer, Alpheus, *Boxing and Self-Defense as taught by the Marshall Stillman principle.* New York, Marshall Stillman Association, 1919. This is one of those books written for the always rich market of growing boys and bank clerks who poignantly feel the need of a means of self-defense.

Geer, Alpheus, *Ju Jitsu Defense Against Violent Attack, Wrestling,* by Marshall Stillman Assoc., 1920. This is another written for the same market.

Geer, Alpheus, *The Manual of the Fist and Self-Defense,* Marshall Stillman, 1918. The first of the commercial books on self-defense.

Gianakaris, George, *Action Drilling in Wrestling* (South Brunswick, New Jersey: A. S. Barnes and Co., 1969).

Gotch, Frank, *Wrestling and How to Train.* Posed by Frank Gotch and Oscar Samuelson. New York, R. R. Fox, 1908. Posed pictures of professional holds. Written for the market. This book at least inspired some growing boys to improve their physical equipment.

Griffin, Marcus, *Fall Guys, the Barnums of Bounce,* Chicago, The Reilly and Lee Co., 1937. Accounts of pro wrestlers.

Grüneisen, Gottfried, *Mein Weg zum Sport,* Zurich, 1947. 235 pg.

Gruhn, Ernest, *The Text Book of Wrestling,* London, Athletic Pub. Co., 1947.

Hackenschmidt, George, *Complete Science of Wrestling,* London, 1909, Health and Strength, Ltd.

Halm, Eugene Wallace John, *The Life and Works of "Farmer" Burns,* Omaha, Nebr, 1911. (not on shelf)

Hikogama, Kōzō, *Sumo, Japanese, Wrestling,* Tokyo. Board of Tourist Industry, Japanese Government Transportation, 1940. Pictures of Champs. Standing throws in Sumo style.

Hitchcock, Edward, *Catch-As-Catch-Can Style, Wrestling,* New York, The American Sports Publishing Co., 1910. Joint author Richard F. Nelligan. 43 p.

Hitchcock, George David, *The Art of American Wrestling,* South Bend, Ind., The Mirror Press, Inc., 1929, 11 p. Modern but meagre.

Hooghe, Romein de "Klare Ondereichlinge de Voortreffelijcke"

Two books by the above author.
1. *Worstel-Konst* Amsterdam, J. J. van Waesherge, 1674.
2. *Der Künstliche Ringer:* Amsterdam, J. Jansson van Waesberge, 1674.

Katulin, A. Borba (Russian). Accounts of Russian wrestling photo's of champs, not instructional.

Kenney, Harold E., and Glenn C. ("Newt") Làw, N.Y. McGraw-Hill 1952. This book is one of the fine books written around this time and has much good material in it. Good arrangement and good illustrations make it a worth while book to have. Good book, all coaches should have it in their library.

LeBow, Guy, *The Wrestling Scene,* N.Y., Homecraft Sports Division, 1950, 96 p.

Leonard, Hugh F., *A Handbook of Wrestling,* 265 pp. N.Y., E. R. Pelton, 1897. This is a beautiful book limited to 300 copies. Excellent posed photographs of

Hugh Leonard and (I think) George Bothner could furnish material for art students. A very complete work of wrestling of that day, showing a multitude of hiplocks, standing grapevine combinations, and much that is still sound free-style wrestling. Every Olympic coach should study this book. Interesting to note that holds were posed on a carpet. Also, references are made as to holds on the carpet and not on the mat. Other books of this time and earlier refer to the carpet. It would be interesting to learn when mats first came into general use. Leonard was coach of the New York Athletic Club. Good for A.A.U. wrestlers.

Liederman, Early Edwin, *The Science of Wrestling and The Art of Ju Jitsu,* N.Y., 1925, 223 p. Excellently bound and illustrated with professional holds. Probably this book was not actually compiled by Liederman who was a weight-lifter and professional muscle man with nationwide publicity. This was produced for the market of hungry physical culturists. Poses by two heavily muscled professionals.

Longhurst, Percy, *Wrestling, London and N.Y.,* F. Warne and Co., 64 p., 1936. Other publication by M. S. Mill Co. Inc., N.Y., 1938, 88 p. Very scanty.

Lundin, Hjalmar, *On the Mat and Off, Memoirs of a Wrestler,* N.Y., Albert Bonner Publishing House, 1937.

McMahon, Donald Vincent, *Fundamentals of High School Wrestling,* Golden Colo., 1951, 189 p. (not on shelf)

Maertz, Richard C., *Wrestling Techniques: Takedowns* (South Brunswick, New Jersey: A. S. Barnes and Co., 1970).

Meyers, John C., *Wrestling from Antiquity to Date,* St. Louis J. C. Meyers, 1931, 130 p.

Muldoon, James, *Professor Muldoon's Wrestling,* N.Y., Street & Smith, 1891. This book is not on the shelf at the Library of Congress. However, it belongs to that era of wrestling before there was a governing body. Strangle holds, hammerlocks, all types of scissor holds were used in the absence of rules. Not as good or as complete as Leonard's book. Muldoon was one of the first great physical culturists.

Oberholzer, Henry A., *Recreative Wrestling,* London, University of London Press, 1949.

*Official Wrestling Guide,* A. S. Barnes Co., N.Y. The Library has these for most of the early years.

Otopalik, Hugo, *Modern Wrestling for High School and College,* N.Y. Chas. Scribner's Sons, 1930. Though a bit meager in material, this book has lots of sound advice to the young wrestler. A good job of rewriting would make this an excellent guide for junior high and high school boys. Good for high school.

Parkyns, Sir Thomas, *The Inn-play or Cornish Hugg Wrestler,* London, printed for T. Weeks at White-hart, 1727. This book is sealed in an envelope and stamped "rare old book." I have not opened it but suspect that the material would be valuable only for its antiquity and novelty (compared with the texts of today). Hiplocks and headlocks as well as certain holds used on clothing or harness were used for throws at this period. The object was to throw the opponent to the ground. Pinning the shoulders was not part of the game.

Pons, Paul, *La Lutte,* Paris, P. Lafitte & Co., 1912. Very meager both in quantity and quality. However, would be interesting to students of foreign wrestling. Almost entirely standing throws, featuring Japanese style.

Robbins, George Sanders, *Frank A. Gotch, World's Champion Wrestler,* J. S. Bowler, Chicago, 1913.

Robbins, G. S., *How to Wrestle (based on work of Gotch),* Chicago, 1934. Max Stein Pub. Co. Pro holds.

Russia   1. Borba Klassicheskaia: programma 1954 (A. Z. Katulin, author).
2. Same as above but dated 1956. Komitet po fizecheskoi kulture i sportu borba.
3. Borba Samba 1954.
With the one exception noted, these Russian books are not illustrated. I doubt that translation would reveal anything new as the Russians seem to have copied information from sources outside their own country.

Sandow, Billy, *Self Defense for the Individual,* Rochester, N.Y., United Lithograph & Printing Co., 1919.

Sandow, Billy and Ed "Strangler" Lewis, *Wrestling,* Kansas City Mo., Sandow-Lewis Inc., 1926.

Shomer, Louis, *Police Ju Jitsu,* Also vital holds in wrestling, N.Y. 1937. Louellen Publishing Co., Inc.

Smith, Ed Wallace, *Professional Wrestling,* N.Y. American Sports Pub. Co., 1932. Spaldings Athletic Library. Some good holds like inside leg work and navy ride shown with pro holds.

Snyder, Juan, *Reglamentos oficiales de luncha libre, greco-romana y levanta-Miento de pesos,* 1941, Tacuba, D. F. Litografia "El Croma." Book of rules, South America.

Sorokin, Nikolai Nikolaevich, 248 p. Borba Klasschehaia, 1956 (Russian). Free style, many standing throws, numerous exercises.

Stone, Henry Attie, *Wrestling, Intercollegiate and Olympic.* This is a mixture of the two styles and includes many good maneuvers in Free-style as well as collegiate. It is well illustrated with good photographs and a discriminating coach can get much good material from it. Organization is good. In fact the whole makeup is good. Only criticism is that it is a bit wordy and more on the old style of formal writing. Certainly one of the better books on wrestling.

Toombs, Frederick R., *How to Wrestle,* N.Y., American Sports Pub. Co., (Spalding's Athletic Library), 1934. While this has some good material, it is outdated and there is nothing in it that cannot be found in any of the more complete works. Several editions showing a good many pros in later ones.

Umbach, Arnold W. and Warren R. Johnson, *Successful Wrestling,* C. V. Mosby St. Louis, 1953. 256 p. This is far ahead of any other book ever written on wrestling. It represents what I believe will be the trend in modern books on sports techniques. As many as eight different drawings are used to show one maneuver from start to finish. Drawings are made from movies and from photographs by a competent professional artist. They are done in contrasting colors and widths of line and there are more than 400 in the book. Dr. Johnson's psychological studies give much food for thought and open an unlimited new field for both coaches and psychologists. Many maneuvers never shown before appear on the pages of this incomparable text. Above all others, this is the book for a coach to have. One of finest on the market.

Umbach, Arnold W. and Warren R. Johnson, *Successful Wrestling* (Dubuque, Iowa: W. C. Brown Company, 1972).

U.S. Bureau of Aeronautics, Navy Dept. *Wrestling,* Annapolis Md. U.S. Naval Institute 1943. Very good but later Navy manuals are better. *One of the best books on the market in 1943.*

V-Five Association of American, Wrestling, Annapolis Md., Naval Institute 1950. Next to Umbach and Johnson's this is the best book on the market. There is a wealth of good new material and the coaches who collaborated to write this are to be congratulated upon a wonderful job. This, too, is a must for any man who is in the coaching game seriously. Especially good are plans for group instruction, training, weightmaking.

*Virginia Rules and Regulations governing boxing and wrestling,* Richmond, Va., 1934.

Vorres, Spyros K., *Wrestle to Win,* Chicago, 1930. Autographed from typewritten copy. Probably one of the poorest jobs of mimeographing ever done. Illustrations apparently traced from photographs which were taken in sunlight with deep shadows requiring a lot of guesswork as to place and shape of legs and arms. Some very poor guesses made.
Yet, *this is the most complete book on wrestling ever written.* Mr. Vorres states at the beginning that he was 12 years in preparing it and I can believe him. It contains just about every hold shown in any book written before and has a wealth of new material that, even at this date, has not appeared in any book. Mr. Vorres shows familiarity with everything pictured, giving complete instructions about how and when to use each hold. He also has a thorough understanding of wrestling psychology. On the strength of this work, I would hazard the guess that no living coach knows more wrestling than Spyros K. Vorres. Much material here not found anywhere else.

Walker, Donald, *Defense Exercises,* London, T. Hurst, 1840.

Zaits, *Borba Klassicheskaia,* 1953, (Russian). Greco-Roman, good drawings.

# Index of Wrestling Nomenclature

185

190